Immigrants and Aliens

Isle of Man Internment Women's Camp: glove making, a camp industry (photograph), 1940 (HO 213/1053)

Immigrants and Aliens

A guide to sources on UK immigration and citizenship

Roger Kershaw and Mark Pearsall

PUBLIC RECORD OFFICE

Public Record Office Readers' Guide No. 22

Public Record Office
Kew
Richmond
Surrey TW9 4DU

ISBN 1 873162 94 4

British Library Cataloguing-in-Publication Data
A catalogue record for this book is available from the British Library

Cover: alien registration card for Marie Bader, 1915 (MEPO 2/1676); party of 585 immigrants from Jamaica arriving at Newhaven, 22 September 1958 (© 1999 Topham Picturepoint)

Printed by The Cromwell Press Ltd, Trowbridge, Wilts.

Contents

Foreword

Where is the immigrant or refugee whose life has not been touched at some point by government? At times the contact has been light, felt almost in passing. On other occasions it has proved heavy, not to say oppressive. It is only to be expected, therefore, that the Public Record Office (PRO) contains a variety of sources on the history of immigration into Britain.

Valuable as they are, these items alone do not provide a full history of this immigration and all its consequences. Historians need to search in other archives for information. That obligation is recognized in this book. There are private papers to be searched. There are also published sources. The autobiographies of people who left their own countries to begin new lives in Britain, whether temporary or permanent, also call for consideration. Sometimes these reflections have derived from the great and the good but in other instances reminiscences have been left by people who lived out of the public limelight and continued 'to blush unseen'. Newspapers, of both the popular and quality kind, constitute another valuable resource. The Press has generally taken a close and at times obsessive interest in the history of immigration. Was the process in the 'public good', however defined? Should it be allowed to continue? On the other side of the coin, space has sometimes been allocated to success stories. Hence stories have been carried on the lives of successful immigrants or refugees, whether in business, culture, or politics, whose lives it is suggested might serve as a role model for others and whose success suggests that Britain is a tolerant country. These press reports have often run in parallel with parliamentary debates.

Historians of immigration certainly cannot afford to neglect *Hansard*. All these aforementioned sources might be regarded as the conventional material of historical research. However, one can also draw upon a rich store of oral testimony, a form of evidence sometimes dismissed by traditional historians. Through such recordings as the cassettes compiled by the Bradford Heritage Recording Unit, it becomes possible for 'groups of people who might have been hidden from history' to make their contributions to an understanding of immigration.

An awareness of that part of British history can only gain from an even further sweep of material. Creative works such as Cecil Hepworth's film *The Aliens' Invasion*, made at the time of Jewish immigration from Russian Poland early in the twentieth century, as well as programmes shown more recently on television, form part of this wider constituency. Radio programmes, collected in the BBC Archives at Caversham, also have their value. So do other forms of creative activity, which have a longer history. The historian of recent immigration can certainly turn to contemporary novels and, beyond doubt, literary works are also relevant for earlier years. Immigrants and refugees have written some of these books. In other instances the literature has emerged from outside these groups but with their presence in mind. Finally, the history of immigration is reflected not only in items which can be read or heard but also in objects which can be seen. The architecture of Britain bears witness to immigration and directly or indirectly reflects the influences of immigrants and refugees. The changing face of Bradford's religious buildings and the now busy mosque on Fournier Street in Spitalfields, which served earlier as a synagogue for the ultra-orthodox and before that as a Huguenot church, are two examples. In other cases the influence of new styles in building has owed much to émigré influences: one thinks straight away of the work of Erno Goldfinger.

There is still a need, however, to consult documents which originate within government. This book provides a valuable service in drawing the attention of researchers to such material. Historians often turn in the first instance towards Home Office files. HO 45 and HO 144 are key file series. Here is a considerable weight of documentary evidence, which helps to reconstruct the process of immigration. However, to limit one's enquiry to this important government department, which is centrally involved in such matters, would be to miss important information generated in other ministries. Foreign Office files help to reconstruct the history of the societies from which Britain drew its European immigrants. As for those immigrant minorities who travelled from the former Imperial territories of the world, details can be found in Colonial Office papers. Indeed, evidence sometimes lurks in these files when there would be every expectation of finding it elsewhere, say within the Home Office series. There are also files from other ministries which deserve attention. War Office papers, such as WO 315, which relate to Poles, and specifically to the Polish Resettlement Corps, the conduit through which many Poles in the shadow of the Second World War entered into civilian life in Britain, constitute one example. However there are others. Owing to the need of immigrants and refugees to secure employment, a large number of documents originated within the Ministry of Labour. Less evidently, but importantly, the Poor Law records of the nineteenth century contain information on the large numbers of Irish migrants who were very much in the sights of policy makers when they drew up the 1834 Poor Law.

Historians who venture to Kew can therefore find a wealth of evidence on immigration. Moreover, anyone who works on such material will soon become aware of several important aspects of the immigration process.

In no sense can the inward movement of groups be regarded as a recent phenomenon. The material in the PRO on medieval Jewry and the Huguenots provides evidence on the much earlier movements of peoples. The official record also picks up on the Dutch who arrived in the wake of William of Orange. There are files, too, on the refugees from France who stayed between 1789 and 1815, some of whose details are contained in Treasury papers. Furthermore, the recent immigration from the Caribbean and the Indian subcontinent, details of which can be found in many files, also needs to be viewed as part of a longer process. In no sense did Black and Asian communities begin their history in Britain in 1945. The proclamation of Elizabeth I against 'Negroes and Blackamoors' and, much later, the tangled question of the so called coloured seaman, details of which can be found in Home Office files, under Nationality and Naturalization, are reminders of this earlier history.

It is not merely the long history of immigration that is revealed by the official record. The files also illustrate the great diversity of groups that have entered the country. Jews and Huguenots, Blacks and Asians, as well as the Dutch, the Irish, the French and the Poles have already been noticed. There is also information on other groups, including the Belgians, the Chinese, the Czechs (see HO 294 on the Czechoslovak Refugee Trust Records, for example), the Germans, the Gypsies from various countries, as well as the Italians. There is also an abundance of files on that mixed bag of refugees recruited after 1945 to help in the rebuilding of Britain. This last group, who went under the name of European Volunteer Workers, included within its ranks Estonians, Latvians, Lithuanians and Ukrainians (on which see LAB 8 and LAB 26, particularly).

This long process, involving a large number of groups, has persisted notwithstanding the increasingly stringent entry controls imposed by government during the twentieth century. In 1900 no barriers stood in the path of foreigners who wanted to enter Britain. Controls had existed between 1793 and 1826, during and in the aftermath of the French Revolutionary Wars. Moreover, the Government assumed the powers to control immigration between 1848 and 1850, once more at a time of a revolutionary upheaval in Europe. However, in the event, no action was taken. Carl Marx, as he was dubbed, was allowed to settle in England (although he was refused naturalization) along with other refugees of varying political persuasions. The following years between 1850 and 1905 constituted a period when entry remained free and unfettered. But in 1905, consequent upon the growing increase in Jewish immigration from Russian Poland, an Aliens Act found its way on to the Statute Book. Henceforth, the entry of aliens became discretionary. Further measures passed in 1914 and particularly in 1919, placed stringent controls on the inward movement of foreigners. As this guide notes, the Poles and other Europeans, whose labour was required to assist in the rebuilding of Britain after 1945, were the first foreigners to be recruited by the Government since 1905. None of these measures affected those peoples intending to come to Britain from the Commonwealth and Empire. However, the open door policy, which existed for much of the twentieth century towards these groups, started to close with the passing of the Commonwealth Immigrants Act in

1962. A further tightening occurred in 1965 and then in 1968 when another Commonwealth Immigrants Act was introduced. In 1971 an Immigration Act, effective from 1973, pulled together the legislation affecting the entry of aliens and Commonwealth immigrants. In that year, 1973, with Britain's entry into the European Community (EC), nationals from other EC member states received the right to enter Britain and to work there. However, later attempts to restrict other immigrations and also to reduce the number of asylum seekers, revealed the continuing intent of successive governments to control movement into the country. Through such developments, some of which can now be reconstructed through the official files, it is possible to trace the emergence of a growing inward-looking stance on immigration.

One final related point. In the course of immigration debates considerable emphasis was laid on the question of numbers. When the Russian Polish Jews arrived, suggestions surfaced that Britain was in danger of being swamped by their presence. Whitechapel would become Jerusalem. A similar emphasis on the weight of numbers allegedly involved in immigration has rippled through into the debates which have taken place since 1945. One recalls this theme in the course of the influential speeches, which Enoch Powell delivered in 1968. Yet the official files on Commonwealth immigration make it clear that when controls were introduced in 1962 against the background of such fears, hardly any worthwhile statistics existed on the immigration which took place by plane or rail from these parts of the world. Sometimes, then, the official files underline the amount of ignorance which lay behind policy decisions.

It is always frustrating to encounter such dead ends. There is a strong tendency when working on public records to believe that all barriers to understanding will be removed. It is a popular belief that governments *must* have known what was happening even if the general public remained in the dark. But it is not merely the failure of government to gather information which results in frustration. In some instances files have been destroyed. The amount of paper created by government departments is immense and the need for constant weeding has to be recognized. In some instances, though, hyperactive weeders untrained in history have wrought their damage. Some sources on the Chinese in the early twentieth century have been thrown away. A number of internment files from the Second World War relating to Austrian, German, and Italian nationals, have been shredded. In both cases, chosen from a bigger list, the quality of the historical record is diminished by such losses.

There is yet another barrier. Even when material has been collected and preserved, it might not be possible to have sight of it. The Public Records Act allows for the retention of material beyond the customary period of thirty years on the grounds of personal sensitivity or for reasons of national security. This problem affects researchers who focus on a number of sensitive areas though access is considered by and at the discretion of the department of origin concerned. In the case of immigration, barriers also exist, for example, regarding the important yet neglected naturalization files. The records from 1923 are retained in the Home Office and requests to view these documents must be made through the Departmental Record Officer.

Notwithstanding such problems, the files in the PRO are of immense interest and some effective use has already been made of these sources. The increase in immigration which followed the Second World War, and especially, but not exclusively that which originated in Africa, Asia and the Caribbean, soon led to a fair number of works by anthropologists, geographers, and sociologists, some of which drew on the official record. An early lead was taken in this activity by scholars from the University of Edinburgh. By contrast, historians were slower to recover the historical processes of immigration. However, piece by piece, doggedly and persistently, the gaps have started to be filled. We are now better informed than several years ago on the complex roots of the nation, glimpsed in part by Daniel Defoe in the early eighteenth century in *The True-Born Englishman*. Even so, greater recognition still needs to be granted to the various processes of migration which have influenced the contours of British history and much work still remains to be done. In these future efforts the official record needs to be fully exploited. By drawing together references to relevant sources in the Public Record Office this guide will assist in these endeavours.

Colin Holmes
Professor of History
University of Sheffield

Acknowledgements

The authors would like to thank fellow colleagues in the PRO for their kind assistance in producing this guide. Particular reference should be made to Dr Mandy Banton, Dr Amanda Bevan, Dr Paul Carter, James Cronan, Dr John Fisher, Guy Grannum, Hilary Jones, Anne Kilminster, Sheila Knight, Aidan Lawes, Sarah Leach, Michael Leydon, Dr Stephen O'Connor, Nick Pinto, Kelvin Smith, Nigel Taylor, and Val Traylen.

We would also like to thank all those local authority record offices and police museums who contributed to Appendix 2, Harriet Jones and Louise Falcini of the London Metropolitan Archives and Professor Colin Holmes for providing the Foreword to the Guide.

Introduction

The purpose of this readers' guide is to help researchers appreciate and understand the wide variety of records concerning immigrants and aliens held at the Public Record Office (PRO) and at other archives. Its intended audience includes genealogists seeking information relating to their own ancestry as well as social and economic historians interested in the history of immigration, and its impact on British society over the past eight hundred years.

The guide aims to explain clearly immigration policy and how it has changed from medieval times. It discusses in depth those government departments responsible for controlling immigration and why certain records were preserved as archives and others were not. Above all, the guide offers guidance to what the records contain and some suggestions on how they might be used.

The structure of the guide allows the user to concentrate on specific key immigration themes, such as those records associated with the physical arrival of aliens (Chapter 3), and those relating to citizenship (Chapter 5). There is also a thematic or subject arrangement looking at specific groups or categories of immigrants in the medieval, early modern and modern eras. A more detailed index at the back of the book allows researchers to dip into the guide at leisure.

The Public Record Office at Kew, in south-west London, houses one of the finest, most complete archives in the world, running unbroken from Domesday Book in 1086 to the present century. It holds the records for the central government of the United Kingdom (primarily of England and Wales, as Scotland and Northern Ireland have their own central record offices), as well as the records of the law courts of England. In addition, it is a major international archive, because of its vast holdings on the former British colonies, and on foreign relations over eight centuries. The Family Records Centre (FRC) in Islington, north London, holds copies of popular family history records held at Kew, together with nineteenth century census returns and records of births, marriages and deaths.

Public records are not normally made available for reading until thirty years after the date of their final creation; thus a file opened in 1960 and closed in 1969 became available in 2000. Exceptions to this rule are noted in the text. Many documents which refer to individuals have much longer closure periods, to safeguard personal confidentiality: an obvious example is the census, which is closed for 100 years. The closure periods for many records are subject to review. Members of the public who can show good cause are entitled to request reviews and re-reviews of document closures.

Records were produced in the course of government and the dispensing of justice. Many people now use them for the wholly different purpose of historical research. Whether your field is family history, social history or economic history, remember that the people who wrote down these records did so because there was an administrative need to do so. As a result, to find the answers we want, we often have to know something of how government and the courts operated, in order to understand better the surviving information.

The PRO bookshop, which runs a mail order service, currently holds about 250 family history titles: for more information write to it or check the PRO web site. Many of the books cited in the bibliography of this guide are available in the PRO, in the Library, the Research Enquiries Room, or the reading rooms. Some can be bought in the shops at Kew and at the FRC. Most can be read in good reference libraries. If it is more convenient, you could try inter-library loan, through your local lending library.

The staff at the PRO and the FRC can help you with advice and guidance, but we can not actually do research for the public. The PRO and the FRC are open reference institutions, where readers have to come to the search rooms to conduct their own research. If this is not possible, then the PRO can supply lists of independent professional researchers or record agents, who will undertake research for a fee. The arrangement between you and the agent will be of a purely private nature and the PRO and FRC can accept no responsibility for any aspect of the arrangements made between record agents and their clients.

The PRO has a very popular web site, at http://www.pro.gov.uk/ where you will find the latest information about the PRO's holdings, opening times, new accessions, publications, bookshop, etc., as well as the current e-mail address. It also contains copies of information leaflets which are sometimes more detailed in their instructions than the information given in this guide. They are designed to be used in the reading rooms, and can be picked up when you arrive, or printed off the web site. The web site also provides access to the PRO catalogue on computer.

The reading rooms at Kew are open to the public until 5 p.m., Monday to Saturday, with late night opening on Tuesday and Thursday until 7 p.m. They open at 9 a.m. except on Tuesdays (10 a.m.) and Saturdays (9.30 a.m.). Documents cannot be ordered until 9.30 a.m. Kew is closed on Sundays, public holidays and during stock-taking (one week, normally the first week in December). There is a restaurant on site, where you can also eat your own food, and a shop.

You will need to get a reader's ticket at the PRO at Kew in order to see original records. This will be issued at Reception when you arrive, on production of some positive means of identification, such as a passport, banker's card, or driving licence or, for foreign nationals, a passport or some other form of national identification document. Children over the age of 14 can be issued with a reader's ticket if they are either accompanied and vouched for by their parents (who have been able to produce their own identification to get a reader's ticket), or if they come with a letter of recommendation from their school, on headed note-paper and signed by the head teacher. We strongly advise readers visiting the office for the first time to arrive in the morning if possible. By doing so (and resources permitting) we will provide you with a 20-minute introduction and tour to help explain our catalogues, document service and document handling issues.

Large bags and coats are not allowed in the research areas at Kew. Lockable hangers are provided for coats, and there are lockers for other belongings. These take a £1 coin, which is returned after use. Pens and coloured pencils are not allowed in the reading rooms, but graphite pencils and laptop computers are: power points are available. Supplies of paper, tracing paper and pencils can be bought in the shops, which also sell magnifying sheets. If you want to trace anything, ask in the Reading Rooms for an acetate sheet to put over the document first. To help preserve the documents, please make use of the foam wedges and covered weights which are supplied – instructions for their use are on display.

The PRO welcomes readers with disabilities. There is a lift to all floors, and the facilities are wheelchair friendly. We have aids for readers with impaired vision, but the totally blind are advised to come with a sighted friend. Equally, if you have mobility difficulties, it may be a good idea to come with a friend, as the PRO is a very large building, and there can be distances to cover between different sources of information. If you contact the PRO in advance, staff can provide wheelchair assistance for the 100 m plus from the car park. You can look at the leaflet on *Physical Access to the Public Record Office and its Services* on the web site, or you can contact the PRO to ask for a copy to be sent to you.

The PRO's address is:

Post	Public Record Office, Ruskin Avenue, Kew, Richmond, Surrey TW9 4DU
Telephone	020 8392 5200
E-mail	enquiry@pro.gov.uk/
Web site	http://www.pro.gov.uk/
Fax	020 8878 8905
Minicom	020 8392 9198

The FRC is open from 10 a.m. on Tuesdays, 9.30 a.m. on Saturdays, and 9 a.m. every other weekday. It closes at 7 p.m. on Tuesday and Thursday, and 5 p.m. on the other days. The FRC is closed on Sundays and public holidays. A reader's ticket is not needed. Pens can be used, and there are power-points for laptops in the PRO searchroom. There is a shop and an eating area in the building, and several places sell meals and sandwiches nearby. There are lockers if you wish to use them: a £1 coin is needed, but is returned after use.

The FRC has ramp access for wheelchairs and a lift to both floors. It also has three parking spaces reserved for disabled readers, which you have to book in advance by ringing 020 7533 6436. There are some motorized microfilm readers with zoom facilities, for disabled readers, and magnifiers are available for printed sources or copies. If you are totally blind or have limited mobility try to come with a sighted or more mobile friend. Once in the building, there is still a considerable amount of walking backwards and forwards during the course of a visit.

The FRC's address is:

Post	Family Records Centre, 1 Myddelton Street, London EC1R 1UW
Telephone	020 8392 5300 – census enquiries
	0151 471 4800 – birth, death and marriage certificate enquiries
Web site	PRO web site at http://www.pro.gov.uk/
	ONS web site at http://www.ons.gov.uk/
Fax	020 8392 5307
Minicom	020 8392 5308

The ONS has a popular web site at http://www.ons.gov.uk/ where you can look under 'Services' for information about ordering certificates, as well as finding out about new services.

An archive, such as the PRO, does not arrange its holdings by subject, but by the original institutional author – the supposed creator of the records. This means that to really get the best out of the sources, you have to have some idea of how the government and courts worked, who was responsible for what kinds of affairs, who was likely to have written to whom, what kind of information might have been collected or retained.

Records in the Public Record Office are divided into 'classes', reflecting as far as possible what they were created for, and how they were used at the time. Each class has its own name and code, and each consists of individual 'pieces', which is what you order to be produced from the storage areas, or what you get yourself from a microfilm or microfiche cabinet. Each piece has a unique reference. This is made up of a lettercode, a class number, and a piece number. For example, the lettercode for

Home Office is HO; the class number for the Aliens Department: General Files and Aliens Naturalization and Nationality Files is 213; and the piece number for Nationality: Policy: Jewish Refuges, 1940 is 44. This gives a complete PRO reference of HO 213/44.

These references can be discovered from the various finding aids in the Public Record Office and via the web using the PRO on-line catalogue.

The Guide to the Content of the PRO (PRO, London, 1998) gives an overview of the history and content of all the records in the care of the PRO. At the PRO several printed copies are available so you can sit and browse at leisure. Copies can also be seen at the FRC (PRO).

The guide occupies several loose-leaf volumes, and is divided into three parts. Part 1 contains the history of government. Part 2 contains class descriptions in alphabetical order of class number for each class. Part 3 is the index to the other two parts. The main kinds of finding aid, below the level of the Guide, are:

List	A list of the pieces comprising a class of records, with dates and simple descriptions (a *descriptive list* gives fuller indications of the contents of each document).
	Lists in the Standard Set of class lists are filed in A4 binders, in alpha-numerical order of lettercode/class number: there are several (colour-coded) sets of the full sequence from A to ZSPC – you are welcome to browse among them, but only the dark green paper set in the research enquiries room is regularly updated.
	Other lists will be found in the Non-Standard Sets or Additional Finding Aids, in the Research Enquiries Room and the Map and Large Room. These are often original or older finding aids, or published works. They each bear a small label on the spine saying which class they refer to.
Introductory note	An introduction to the contents of a class, explaining why the records were created, and what they contain. These exist for all medieval, early modern and legal classes, for most very modern classes, and for some other classes.
	They are usually printed on green paper, and are filed with the class lists in what is known as the Standard Set of class lists.
	This is the full set of paper lists, in alphabetical order.
Calendar	A précis, usually in English, full enough to replace the original documents for most purposes. The documents have been published in date order in many, but not all, calendars.
Publications	The PRO publishes readers' guides and handbooks. These are the specialist guides to particular records, referred to in this book.
Transcript	A full text.
Index	Alphabetically arranged references to people, places or subjects mentioned in the records.

As well as the traditional methods described above, you will by the end of 2000 have the option of searching through the whole combined catalogue (PROCAT) of the guide and lists on computer. This will eventually be accessible over the web and will contain record descriptions of all PRO holdings. An interim version of the lists, known as the 'On-line Lists', is in use at the time of writing. As well as via the web, this can be seen at Kew and at the FRC.

You may find that you need to operate the two systems of searching together until PROCAT is completed.

The PRO Library has not been open to the public for very long, and it is still a rather under-used resource. It has excellent sets of periodicals and journals, for all kinds of history.

The Library has the indexes to *The Times* and the Parliamentary Papers (from 1801) on CD-ROM, as well as several other useful CD-ROMs. These can produce extraordinary amounts of information – the Parliamentary Papers in particular are full of details, and using the index on a keyword search can turn up all kinds of published returns of people marginally involved in government, or giving evidence on subjects of social concern.

The legislative framework

1.1 Denizen or native?

If you were born within the king's allegiance you were his subject; if you were born outside the king's allegiance you were a stranger or alien owing allegiance to another prince. In the medieval period the concepts of state and statehood and nationality were not clearly defined. The king had subjects in England who were English, but he also had possessions in France and subjects who were French.

With the loss of territories on the continent, those born there outside the king's allegiance were foreigners. In the fourteenth century parliament legislated to confirm that the king's children born beyond the sea could inherit and were his subjects, as too were children born abroad of parents in the king's service. In 1351 an Act was passed to give this effect and declared all children born beyond the sea to parents within the king's allegiance to be capable of inheriting land and property. This was confirmed by a further Act of 1368.

The making of a foreign subject into a native subject was not covered by this legislation. The first instance of making a foreigner into a native subject was in 1295, in the form of a grant by Edward I by which the king held a man to be an Englishman and required that all others in the kingdom should also consider him to be an Englishman. This was the beginning of the concept of naturalization, though there was no formal grant by letters patent or Act of parliament.

The distinction between denization by letters patent of the king, and naturalization by Act of parliament did not at first exist and took time to evolve. Petitions could be made to parliament and parliament would agree to letters patent being issued. Conversely, grants by letters patent could be confirmed by Act of parliament.

The first instance of a distinction is in the case of Henry Hansforth in 1431 when parliament passed a bill giving him full rights of a native subject. The king amended the provisions so that he would pay customs as would a stranger, that is a foreigner. This development helps to explain the subsequent emergence, during the Tudor period, of two main distinctions between the denization and naturalization – the granter and the rights conferred *see* Section 5.1.3. This dual system continued after the Tudor period. In the seventeenth century, the terms denization and naturalization were still often used interchangeably and the term denization can be found in Acts of parliament.

1.2 A chronology of key legislation

Before the eighteenth century, there was little general legislation regarding citizenship, and those laws that were passed tended to relate only to restrictions imposed on foreign merchants and craftsmen, or immigrants, whether denizens or naturalized. Nevertheless, the early legislation outlined below may still be considered important in helping to shape the general laws of nationality which emerged later. This list should not be considered comprehensive, but includes Acts resulting in the creation of records surviving in the PRO.

1.2.1 A chronology of English and British law

1523   An Act (14 & 15 Hen. VIII c. 2) to regulate stranger craftsmen.

1529   An Act (21 Hen. VIII c. 16) ratified a decree of Star Chamber requiring all aliens (including denizens) to swear allegiance to the king – this condition was, by an Act (7 Jas. I c. 2) in 1609, extended to all naturalized aliens under the influence of anti-Catholic feeling. The Act of 1529 was also designed to control craftsmen and regulate their relationship to the City livery companies.

1540   An Act (32 Hen. VIII c. 16) strengthened the law relating to stranger denizens and patents of denization.

1660–1710   Formulating cohesive naturalization legislation proved difficult. Between 1660 and 1710 attempts were made to pass through parliament a true naturalization bill, one that would apply to all aliens. When the tide of Huguenot refugees became a flood, the forms of denization procedure were relaxed and leave was granted by order in Council for the wholesale grants of denizations without the payment of any fee.

1701   The Act of Succession (12 & 13 Will. III. c. 2) provided in clause 3 that no person born out of England, Scotland or Ireland although naturalized or made a denizen should be capable of being of the Privy Council, of parliament or of holding office or trust under the Crown or of having grants of land under the Crown.

1708   The Act for Naturalization of Foreign Protestants (7 Anne c. 5) made provision for the flood of Huguenot refugees by providing a simpler method for naturalizing foreigners. In passing the Act, parliament recognized the opportunity for increasing wealth by simplifying the process of naturalization. The Act enabled aliens to be declared natives on taking the oaths of allegiance and signing the declaration in the Courts of England, Scotland or the Quarter Sessions. They also needed to produce proof that they had within three months before swearing the oaths, taken the Sacrament in some Protestant or reformed congregation within the United Kingdom. The Act was repealed in 1710, apart from one clause which allowed for children born abroad of natural born subjects to be taken to be natural born subjects themselves.

1731 By an Act (4 Geo. II c. 21) children whose fathers were or were to become naturalized British citizens would themselves be taken to be natural born subjects. Previously, it was required that both father and mother had to have been natural born subjects.

1773 By a further Act (13 Geo. III c. 21) the principal outlined above was extended to the children of the children affected by the 1731 Act.

1793 An Aliens Act (33 Geo. III c. 4) was passed by the government requiring aliens to register by means of declarations signed at ports of entry. A superintendent of aliens was appointed and an aliens office created. Further acts were passed in 1816 and 1826.

1836 The Aliens Act (6 & 7 Will. IV c. 11) led to a reorganization which incorporated the Aliens Office into the Home Office. It introduced some relaxation in the system of registration but continued the requirement that masters of vessels and aliens should make a declaration on arrival.

In general, late eighteenth and nineteenth century naturalization legislation resulted in lightening the disabilities of naturalized aliens and simplifying and cheapening the forms of admission.

1844 The Naturalization Act (7 & 8 Vict. c. 66) provided that every alien residing in Great Britain with intent to settle should present a memorial to the Secretary of State stating age, trade and duration of residence. Thereupon the Secretary of State would issue to the memorialist a certificate granting rights of a natural born subject with the exception of the right of being of the Privy Council or parliament. The Act maintained the taking of the oath of allegiance and Act of Succession and provided that any woman married to a natural born or naturalized person was deemed naturalized herself. It further stipulated that applicants wishing to become naturalized citizens should state their intention to reside and settle in Great Britain.

1870 The Naturalization Act (33 & 34 Vict. c. 14) laid down a qualification period so that applicants had to have resided in the United Kingdom or served the Crown for a period of at least five years before being eligible for consideration.

1905   The Aliens Act (5 Edw. VII c. 13) provided for a new system of immigration control and registration and placed responsibility for all matters of immigration and nationality on the Home Secretary.

1914   The Aliens Registration Act (4 & 5 Geo. V c. 12). As the name suggests, this Act made mandatory the registration with the police of all aliens over the age of 16.

1914   The First World War brought further change in naturalization legislation. Under the British Nationality and Status Act (4 & 5 Geo. V c. 17) the statutory qualification of applicants was extended to record that applicants must be of good character and must have an adequate knowledge of English.

1948   The British Nationality Act 1948 (11 & 12 Geo. VI c. 56) made provision for different categories of certificates for the registration of British citizenship for British subjects or citizens of Ireland, the Channel Islands, Isle of Man, any colony, protectorate, and certain protected states. These provisions, together with those for the general Acts of Nationality in 1844, 1870 and 1914, can be found in Appendix 3.

1962   The Commonwealth Immigrants Act (10 & 11 Eliz. II c. 21) required all Commonwealth citizens seeking employment in Britain to qualify for an employment voucher. This limited the right of entry to the United Kingdom; those with passports not issued in Britain were obliged to hold a work permit to secure entry.

1968   The Commonwealth Immigrants Act (1968 c. 9) further tightened controls. Potential immigrants were now required to prove that they themselves were born in the United Kingdom, or that their parents or grandparents had been.

1971   The Immigration Act (1971 c. 77) which came into force on 1 January 1973 brought Commonwealth citizens into line with citizens of foreign countries in so far as employment was concerned. It therefore required Commonwealth citizens to have prospective employers in order to come to the United Kingdom for employment. By order of this Act, nationals of countries within the European Union have not required work permits.

2 Post-war immigration and British citizenship

2.1 European immigration

The largest group of Europeans in Britain after the end of the Second World War was the Poles – over 160,000 by 1950 (*see* 3.4.4). The Poles and other eastern European workers in the late 1940s were the only group since the Aliens Act 1905 to be recruited and settled from Europe. This resulted largely through an economic need to rebuild but also as a way of showing gratitude to the Poles for their distinctive wartime effort. The post-war Labour government actively recruited foreign labour from Poland, eastern Europe, and Ireland.

2.2 Colonial immigration, pre-1948

Before the Second World War there already existed small communities of black people in ports such as Liverpool, Cardiff, Manchester, and London. These settlements had been established mainly by colonial seamen, particularly during the First World War – *see* Section 6.3. On the outbreak of the Second World War many colonists were recruited for war service in the United Kingdom and many stayed in this country after the end of the war.

Indians did not come to Britain in any number before about 1950. However, at the Oriental and India Office Collections, British Library (for address *see* Appendix 4), there are scattered references in Public and Judicial Department annual files (BL references: L/P & J/6 and L/P & J/7) to the provision that was made in the nineteenth and early twentieth centuries for destitute Indians in the UK. These people, who include seamen and discharged servants, appear to have become stranded in Britain and so were, effectively, immigrants. The indexes to these records include names of individuals.

2.3 Colonial immigration, 1948–62

Before 1962, there existed no government machinery to prevent colonial migration. Under the British Nationality Act 1948, certificates of British nationality could be granted to subjects of any British colony or protectorate and Home Office copies of these records can be found in the class of records, HO 334. *See* Section 2.5 for further information about these records.

In response to a continuing lack of unskilled labour, the British government in 1948 created a working party. Their aim was to make use of the unemployed immigrants from the British colonies, especially those from the West Indies. This post-war surplus of manpower was due to the continued residence of West Indian servicemen, who were now facing prejudice from white employers. The committee recognized the serious unemployment situation in the West Indies. The population of Jamaica was expanding at a rate that could not easily be contained by the economy. Many West Indians stayed in Britain after wartime service and those that returned home often found the conditions and opportunities there poor and found it difficult to re-adjust to such limitations. The committee was concerned about the discrimination that black workers would face and the difficulties involved in assimilating them. It therefore recommended no large scale immigration of male colonial workers. The committee preferred European volunteer workers as they were subject to strict labour controls and could be prosecuted or deported if they broke their conditions of recruitment. The committee was more sympathetic to the recruitment of female colonial workers, noting the serious labour shortages in domestic employment, the Health Service and textile industries. The findings of this committee can be found in LAB 26/226.

The Commonwealth Immigrants Act 1962 would eventually put an end to easy immigration from the colonies in the aftermath of the Second World War – *see* Section 2.4.

The majority of migrants from the Indian sub-continent arrived in Britain in the 1950s and 1960s. Asians expelled from Kenya with British passports settled in the UK in 1967.

2.3.1 Lists of colonial immigrants

The only lists of colonial immigrants are the inwards passenger lists in BT 26, which survive up to and including 1960. These give the names of all passengers arriving in the UK where the ship's voyage began at a port outside Europe and the Mediterranean Sea. For further information relating to such records, *see* Section 4.2.1.

Many colonial migrants arrived in the UK by plane or by train, entering Victoria, via Calais and Dover, after disembarking from their ships on the Continent, from such ports as Marseilles, Genoa and Vigo. The PRO does not hold arrival details for such migrants.

2.3.2 Colonial records

Individual colonies set up schemes and committees to deal with the administration of emigration to the United Kingdom. Records of general migration schemes may be found among the classes CO 323: Colonies: General: Original Correspondence and CO 1032: Colonial Office: Defence and General Department and successors:

Registered Files. Correspondence relating to schemes in specific colonies may be found under relevant CO (Colonial Office) correspondence classes. Papers include schemes set up to deal with emigration from the colonies, the employment, recruitment, and the welfare of specific categories of workers, studies of migration movements, and reports on how easily colonial migrants settled in the UK.

DO 35: Dominions Office and Commonwealth Relations Office: Original Correspondence and DO 175: General and Migration records include files relating to measures for control of immigration from the colonies during the 1950s. Later records (from 1967) can be found in FCO 50: Foreign and Commonwealth Office: General and Migration Department.

See Source Sheet 30 for sources of records relating to West Indian immigration and labour.

2.3.3 *Central government response to colonial immigration*

During the 1950s, the Cabinet arranged reviews of colonial immigration. Without any legislation or real control of colonial immigration, there were increasing concerns about employment and law and order. Cabinet Minutes: CAB 128 and Cabinet Memoranda: CAB 129 include references to such reviews and these records are on open access in both the Microfilm Reading Room and Research Enquiries Room. Cabinet Committees were set up specifically to look at the immigration of British subjects into the United Kingdom. CAB 130/61 consists of papers relating to concerns with the increase of immigrants from dependent territories to Britain since 1945, which contributed to unemployment. The committee considered laws governing the entry of aliens, the measures that could be adopted to control this trend and the policy issues involved. Most of the immigrants came from West Africa, the West Indies, Somaliland, Aden and the Mediterranean colonies.

As there was no central government mechanism to prevent colonial immigration, the Home Office found it difficult to estimate reliably annual net colonial immigration. Shipping and air transport passenger lists did not distinguish reliably between intending migrants and tourists. For the years 1955–60, the Home Office estimated a net influx of 160,000 West Indian migrants, compared with 33,000 from India and 17,000 from Pakistan.

Home Office general files relating to establishment matters, policy, disturbances, and casework on a variety of immigration and aliens issues can be found in HO 213, HO 325, HO 352, HO 355, HO 367 and HO 394.

Ministry of Labour files relating to the employment, welfare and training of colonial migrants can be found in the classes LAB 8, LAB 13 and LAB 26. These include many papers on Commonwealth migration and labour, including reports and papers on the Commonwealth Immigrants Act 1962.

Metropolitan Police files relating to attitudes towards colonial migrants, the integration of colonial migrants into local communities and issues relating to law and order can be found in MEPO 2. Cases investigated by the Race Relations Board are in CK 2.

2.4 Colonial immigration: post-1962

The Commonwealth Immigrants Act 1962 was the culmination of more than a decade of mounting public pressure for some restriction of immigration from the British colonies. The fear of control drew in larger numbers of migrants from the Caribbean in 1961 and 1962. The Commonwealth Immigrants Bill, which passed through the Commons in July 1962, required all Commonwealth citizens seeking employment in Britain, to qualify for a voucher. Special emphasis was laid on the control of unskilled workers. The resulting Commonwealth Immigrants Act 1962 limited the right of entry to the United Kingdom; those with passports not issued in Britain were obliged to hold a work permit to secure entry. After 1962 there was never again to be a return to the unrestricted policies of the post-war years. The Commonwealth Immigrants Act 1968 further tightened controls. Potential immigrants were now required to prove that they themselves had been born in the United Kingdom, or that their parents or grandparents had been.

Records of the Commonwealth Relations Office that dealt with the Overseas Migration Board are in the MIG series in DO 35, DO 175, and FCO 50. The Board was purely advisory in function. The Board consisted of three members of parliament, and the joint secretaries were from the Ministry of Labour and the Commonwealth Relations Office. Officials from both these departments attended Board meetings as observers. DO 175 includes records of the Migration and General Department of the General Division, 1962–4.

Vouchers for the employment of Commonwealth citizens were issued under the Commonwealth Immigrants Acts, 1962 and 1968. The vouchers were issued in two categories: category A for Commonwealth citizens with a definite offer of a job, and category B for those who held certain specified professional qualifications. Application for a category A voucher was made by the prospective employer. Except for Malta and the Dependent Territories they were issued for: those holding professional qualifications and managerial and executive staff; skilled craftsmen and experienced teachers; specialized clerical and secretarial staff; and those coming for work which, in the opinion of the Secretary of State for Employment, was of substantial economic and social value to the United Kingdom.

Vouchers were not issued if the vacancy offered could be filled by resident labour. Special arrangements existed for the admission, without vouchers, of doctors and dentists. Only a limited number of vouchers were issued annually, based on fixed quotas for the various countries of the Commonwealth.

LAB 42 consists of specimen applications. All pieces in this class are open to public inspection following a re-review in 1998.

The issue of vouchers was brought to an end by the Immigration Act 1971, which came into force on 1 January 1973. The effect of this Act was to bring Commonwealth citizens in line with citizens of foreign countries, in so far as employment was concerned, which meant that Commonwealth citizens had to have a prospective employer in order to come to this country to work.

LAB 48 contains specimen applications from aliens, 1968 to 1972, and from 1973 onwards, from both aliens and Commonwealth citizens. The majority of these records are open to public inspection following a re-review in 1998.

2.5 Registration of British citizenship documents 1948–69

These documents are generally known as 'R' certificates and refer to registrations of British citizenship declared by a British subject or citizen of the Republic of Ireland or of the Channel Islands, Isle of Man, a colony, a protectorate or a protected state, or a UK Trust Territory. The distinctions between the various 'R' categories are listed in Appendix 3. Usually, the certificates provide the applicant's (and spouse's) name, address and date and place of birth, the applicant's father's name, and the nationality of the applicant.

The PRO does not hold any name indexes to the registration of British citizenship certificates. Indexes are held by the Immigration and Nationality Department in Liverpool. These are arranged alphabetically and give name, date of birth, certificate number and date when the certificate was granted. In order to trace an 'R' certificate for which the certificate number is unknown, it is necessary to contact the Immigration and Nationality Department (for address *see* Appendix 4) in writing. The certificates at the PRO are arranged by certificate number, so, unless this is known, researchers may need to contact the Department in writing prior to visiting the PRO. Certificates issued after 1969 are available via the Home Office (for address *see* Appendix 4), though restrictions apply to those issued less than 30 years ago.

'R' certificates were issued under the British Nationality Act 1948 and duplicate Home Office copies may be found in the class HO 334. The certificates enabled colonial workers and families to migrate with ease to Britain between 1948 and 1962.

3 Aliens, spies, refugees, internees and deportees in the twentieth century

3.1 General sources

Immigration in the twentieth century involved a wide range of people who for economic, cultural or social reasons took a decision to leave their native countries with the intention of staying in Britain temporarily or permanently. In addition, Britain witnessed the arrival of refugees from political or religious oppression in their own countries. Britain's traditional open-door policy on immigration was significantly tested in the course of the twentieth century as unemployment grew. Many refugees who came into the country came to be absorbed into British society – *see* Chapter 7.

One major source for immigration records of the twentieth century is the Cabinet Office records, which include the conclusions and papers of the Cabinet and War Cabinets and their Committees. Many of these records are available as copies in the Research Enquiries Room or on microfilm in the Microfilm Reading Room. Cabinet Minutes and Conclusions can be found in CAB 23 for 1916–39, CAB 65 for 1939–45, and in CAB 129 after 1945. Cabinet Papers or Memoranda can be found in CAB 37 for 1880–1916, CAB 24 for 1916–39, CAB 66 for 1939–45 and CAB 129 after 1945. The PRO has published several books about the papers of the Cabinet Office which describe these records in great detail. These handbooks include:

No. 4	*List of Cabinet Papers, 1880–1914*	(HMSO 1964)
No. 6	*List of Papers of the Committee for Imperial Defence to 1914*	(HMSO 1964)
No. 9	*List of Cabinet Papers, 1915–1916*	(HMSO 1966)
No. 11	*The Records of the Cabinet Office to 1922*	(HMSO 1966)
No. 15	*The Second World War: A Guide to Documents in the PRO*	(HMSO 1993)
No. 17	*The Cabinet Office to 1945*	(HMSO 1975)

All the handbooks are available for consultation in the Research Enquiries Room. As some are out of print it may be necessary to refer to the CD-ROM *PROfiles* and the CD-ROM on the Macmillan years. Both are available for consultation in the Library.

Other central government records concerning aliens and refugees may be found among Prime Minister's Office (PREM) papers. Correspondence and papers from 1916 to 1940 are in PREM 1. Files from 1940 to 1945 are in PREM 3. General correspondence and papers from 1945 to 1951 are in PREM 8 and from 1951 to 1964 in PREM 11. The series continues after 1964 in PREM 13.

General policy matters and files concerning aliens, refugees, internees and deportees in the twentieth century can be found among Home Office classes, specifically HO 45 (Registered Papers) and HO 144 (Registered Papers: supplementary), mainly under the subject headings 'Aliens', 'Nationality', and 'War' for the period before 1920 (*see* Appendix 1 for an explanation on how to use these classes) and HO 213 (Aliens Department: general and aliens' naturalization and nationality files) for the period thereafter. All three classes contain general policy files and deal with the definition of British and foreign nationality, immigration, refugees, internees and prisoners of war, deportation and related subjects. Some pieces in HO 144 and HO 213 are closed for 75 or 100 years and some are still retained by the Home Office.

Other related classes containing general policy files for these subjects include HO 352, HO 355 and HO 367. In 1962 the Aliens Department was merged with the Naturalization and Nationality Division and renamed the Immigration and Nationality Department and files for this period are destined for HO 394, though (at the date of publication) these records are still with the Home Office.

LAB 8 and LAB 26 consist of files relating to general policy matters and welfare matters dealt with by the Ministry of Labour. They include a variety of subjects including accommodation, particularly for immigrant post-Second World War refugees and other foreign nationals, the recruitment of foreigners to work in Britain, hostels, housing estates for Polish workers (*see* Section 3.4.4.4), clubs and other recreational centres.

The indexes to the general correspondence of the Foreign Office (FO) also contain information relating to the arrival of aliens and refugees in the twentieth century. The period 1906 to 1919 is covered by a card index in the Research Enquiries Room. From 1920 to 1951 the index is in the form of printed volumes, also held here, and for the years 1952, 1953 and 1959 there are similar non-published departmental indexes also held in the Research Enquiries Room. These indexes mainly refer to papers in FO 371: Political Departments, but some refer to other departments, such as FO 369: Consular Department, FO 370: Library and Research Departments, FO 372: Treaty Department and FO 395: News Department. For the years 1954 to 1958 and from 1960 to 1966 there are no detailed indexes in these classes and it is necessary to consult the relevant class lists to access the records. From 1967 to October 1968, when the Foreign and Commonwealth Office was formed, the political departments of the Foreign Office operated a common registry with the Commonwealth Office and the Diplomatic

Service Administration Office, and records from this period can be found in various FCO classes by department.

Records of the Metropolitan Police Office in MEPO 2: Correspondence and Papers and MEPO 3: Correspondence and Papers, Special Series include a selection of files relating to aliens, refugees and internees. Many concern general matters dealt with by the Aliens Registration Office of the Metropolitan Police Office. This was set up following the passing of the Aliens Registration Act 1914 which called for the registration with the police of aliens over the age of 16. Other files deal with specific issues such as alien registration (*see* Section 3.2.2), and internment (*see* Section 3.5).

3.2 Aliens

In the early years of the twentieth century, the British government placed very little emphasis on the control or registering of immigrants, and there is a corresponding paucity of records for this period. As the 1903 Royal Commission on Alien Immigration found, only deck passengers were subject to any kind of examination by local customs officers. Once landed, aliens were subject to no further restrictions and, as no registration was called for, the only data which could be obtained concerning the alien population was that which might be sifted from census returns:

Census year	Population of UK	Aliens shown in returns
1881	34,884,848	135,640
1891	37,732,922	219,523
1901	41,458,721	286,952

The increase of the alien population in the years 1881–1901 was estimated to be 150,000.

The report of the Commission stated that the lack of immigration control led to the spread of disease, criminals and anarchists. All this put added strain on the resources of the communities in which most poor aliens made their homes, such as the East End of London. The concerns of the Royal Commission resulted in the Aliens Act 1905.

The outbreak of the First World War naturally necessitated tighter legislation on aliens. The Aliens Registration Act 1914, as the name suggests, made mandatory the registration with the police of all aliens over the age of 16. For the first time, such registration provided the government with accurate information concerning the profession, age, race and location of aliens and assisted the Security Services (MI5), *see* Section 3.2.2, in carrying out their work.

With the enactment of the Aliens Order of 1920, the Immigration Branch of the Home Office was set up and the country was divided into districts: Newcastle, Hull, Harwich, London, Dover, Southampton, and Bristol, each supervised by an Inspector. Scotland and Northern Ireland were looked after by a Chief Immigration Officer, stationed at Glasgow.

Their authority was to enforce immigration legislation and control at ports in the inter-war period, until humanitarian considerations in the 1930s raised by the influx of refugees from Nazi Germany, led to a relaxation of the Aliens Order and the entire nature of the Immigration Service's work altered with the outbreak of the Second World War.

3.2.1 Home Office records

A personal file would have been opened on any alien who had contact with the Home Office and the file would have been maintained from the initial visa or employment application through to an application for naturalization. HO 382: Aliens Department: Aliens Personal Files contains only two files (William Joyce – Lord Haw Haw – and Mikhail Borodin). These files were selected because the individuals are famous. HO 382 will contain more cases selected either because the individual is famous and the file may add to what is known of them (i.e. sources for biographers), or as a specimen file to illustrate how the Home Office handled various aspects of immigration control and how immigration policy was applied in actual cases.

The selection of pre-Second World War files has been generous to show how the Home Office handled those refugees from Nazism who did not settle here. There will also be a relatively large number of Cold War files – mainly of socialist refugees who lived here during the Second World War and returned home, only to return as refugees from Stalinism: many of them failed to obtain naturalization.

The file series was opened in 1934 but occasionally has older papers (6-figure series) attached, with a handful dating back to the 1880s. Some files continue until the 1990s. A selection of files has been made from files opened between 1934 and 1960, though files for the period 1960–75 will be reviewed during 2000 and 2001. Closure of these files will be on the basis of individual review and will be for thirty years or the lifetime of the individual concerned, whichever is longer. The Home Office are reviewing some of the famous cases with a view to opening them in 2000.

HO 405 will be the class of records for all the post-1934 applications for naturalization *see* Section 5.4.6.

Until all the above files have been transferred and opened, the Home Office will continue to respond to enquiries from researchers as at present (*see* Appendix 4 for address).

It will be many years before all the files are at the PRO and many more before they are fully available.

HO 5 includes out-letters and entry books of the Home Office and the Aliens Office relating to issues concerning aliens, such as applications for naturalization and the issuing of alien certificates – *see* Chapter 4. The class covers the period 1794 to 1921, though many of the pieces are not indexed by name.

3.2.2 Police records

The requirement for aliens to register with the police was introduced under the provisions of the Aliens Registration Act 1914; it was renewed by the Aliens Restriction (Amendment) Act 1919 and the Immigration Act 1971. The legislation gave to the government the power to require aliens to register with the police giving detailed particulars including name, address, marital status, employment or occupation, employer's name and address, a photograph, and to pay a registration fee. A registered person was required also to register changes of address, marital status, nationality, and employment or occupation. In return the alien received a police certificate of registration.

Registers of aliens, where they survive, can be found locally at either county record offices or police archives (*see* Appendix 2). No central register of aliens survives, though HO 45/10831/326287 and HO 45/11522/287235 consist of policy and administrative papers in respect of the register. Sample registration cards issued by the Aliens Registration Office of the Metropolitan Police are due for transfer to the PRO in the class MEPO 35, during 2000 or 2001 and, subject to funding, these records will be made available on microfiche in the Microfilm Reading Room. The cards represent several hundred cases from those of the hundreds of thousands of aliens who resided in London and cover the period 1884 to 1989, though there is a heavy concentration around the late 1930s, as Germans and east Europeans fled the Nazi persecutions. Normally cards were destroyed ten years after an alien was naturalized, departed from the UK or died, whichever first applied. The information provided on the cards includes full name, date of birth, date of arrival in the UK, employment history, address, marital status, details of any children, and date of naturalization, with Home Office reference if applicable. The cards usually include at least one photograph and for some cases there are continuation cards.

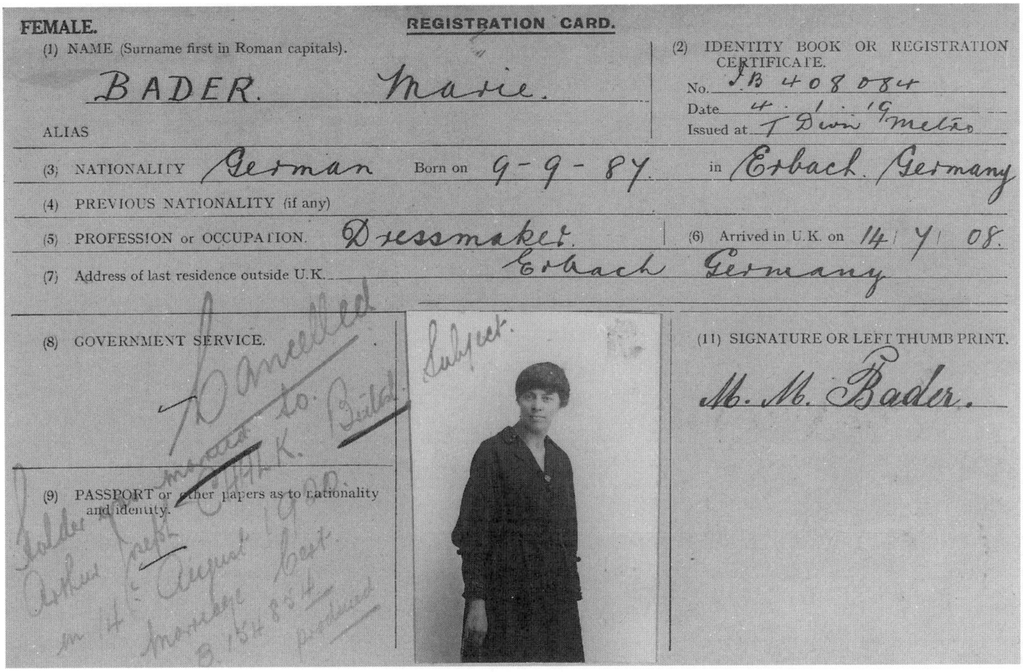
FEMALE. REGISTRATION CARD.

(1) NAME (Surname first in Roman capitals). BADER. Marie.

ALIAS

(2) IDENTITY BOOK OR REGISTRATION CERTIFICATE.
No. J.B 408084
Date 4. 1. 19
Issued at T Divn Metro

(3) NATIONALITY German Born on 9-9-87. in Erbach / Germany

(4) PREVIOUS NATIONALITY (if any)

(5) PROFESSION or OCCUPATION. Dressmaker. (6) Arrived in U.K. on 14/ 7/ 08.

(7) Address of last residence outside U.K. Erbach Germany

(8) GOVERNMENT SERVICE. Cancelled

(9) PASSPORT or other papers as to nationality and identity.

(11) SIGNATURE OR LEFT THUMB PRINT. M. M. Bader.

Figure 1 Alien identity registration card for Marie Bader, 1915 (MEPO 2/1676)

Policy papers relating to the administration of the Aliens Registration Act 1914 can be found in MEPO 2: Correspondence and Papers and MEPO 3: Correspondence and Papers, Special Series. Some records include names of aliens. For example, MEPO 3/2435 contains returns and reports on aliens holding liquor licences or employed in licensed houses in London Metropolitan Police districts during the First World War. Also, MEPO 2/1796 includes a list of German nationals resident in London who applied for the return of their property sequestrated by the government during the First World War.

3.2.3 Ministry of Labour records

LAB 8 and LAB 26 consist of files relating to general policy matters and welfare matters dealt with by the Ministry of Labour. They include a variety of subjects, such as accommodation, particularly for immigrant post-Second World War refugees and other foreign nationals, the recruitment of foreigners to work in Britain, hostels, housing estates for Polish workers (*see* Section 3.4.4.4), clubs and other recreational centres.

Specimen applications from aliens for work permits can be found in LAB 900/1 and LAB 48. The latter consists of applications from aliens between 1968 and 1975. The majority of these records were opened to public inspection in 1998 following a re-review – *see* Section 2.4.

3.3 Spies

The history of the Security Services dates from October 1909 when, following on a decision of the Committee of Imperial Defence (CID), Captain V. G. W. Kell was appointed, under the Director of Military Operations at the War Office, to conduct enquiries into German espionage in the United Kingdom.

As mentioned in Section 3.1, shortly before the First World War a register was compiled of all aliens suspected of espionage in the United Kingdom and lists were prepared and handed to chief constables concerned of those persons who were known or suspected to be German agents. When war was declared these persons were arrested.

The work of the Security Service (MI5) from its formation in 1909 up to the end of the First World War was divided into a number of branches, many of which dealt with issues concerning aliens. All of the records described below can be found in KV 1: The Security Service: First World War Historical Reports and Other Papers, available in the Microfilm Reading Room, and have been published on CD-ROM as *M.I.5 1909–1919: the first ten years* (PRO, 1998).

Branch A, formed in 1917, was responsible for examining the antecedents of friendly aliens, mostly refugees from the war zones, who were needed to work in the munitions factories. KV 1/13–14 consist of reports, appendices and indexes on aliens employed on war service, 1916–19.

Branch E, established in May 1915, was responsible for the control of entry through British ports, as well as alien seamen (60,000 of whom were processed between June and November 1918). These records are in KV 1/20–34 with specific reference to alien seamen in KV 1/35.

Branch F (KV 1/35–8) was the main preventative branch of MI5 and its role was to formulate policy on measures for controlling access to classified information and to promote the necessary emergency legislation (Official Secrets Act, Aliens Restriction Orders, etc.). With the Home Office, Branch F was responsible for the development of policy on the control of aliens and the detention of suspects under the Defence of the Realm Regulation 17B, which at its peak involved the detention of some 32,000 people deemed to be a threat to national security.

Branch G (KV 1/39–48) investigated espionage cases. Prior to the war MI5 had identified 36 German agents operating in Britain and 21 suspect spies were arrested at the outbreak of war. During the war the branch continued its investigative work and uncovered over 30 more agents sent to Great Britain by the German Intelligence Services. The records in this series include detailed reports on individual cases – an index to names can be found in KV 1/47.

Branch H (KV 1/49–63) constituted the Secretariat and the administrative branch of MI5, including the Registry. KV 1/65–7 relate specifically to control of aliens including CID sub-committee reports and MI5 policy matters.

Personal files of enemy agents from the First World War (including those for Mata Hari and Roger Casement) and the Second World War (including the MI5 files on Hess) and a number of files revealing the role of Juan Garcia Pujol (GARBO) in the deception operations of the Second World War can be found in KV 2: The Security Service: Personal Files (PF Series) and KV 4: The Security Service: Second World War Historical Reports. These records provide important information on the history of the service, its relations with other government departments and organizations, interrogation techniques and the preparation of cases for prosecution of enemy agents

Figure 2 Mata Hari – the glamorous First World War spy (KV 2/2)

in the courts. The files of the agents themselves not only shed light on the methods of the service and the various holding centres, but also provide direct information about the individuals and their life histories (in various versions). The personal files also include, in general, accounts of the preparation of cases for prosecution; usually at the Central Criminal Court (Old Bailey), but occasionally by court martial, and unusually, a full transcript of proceedings in court.

Section histories of interrogation camps can also be found in KV 4. KV 4/8 contains a report on the operations of Camp 020 and Camp 020 – R(B1E) in connection with the interrogation of enemy agents during the Second World War. This typescript history provides an overview of the two camps and an analysis of the accommodation and conditions of life for those detained there and the methods of interrogation employed. Camp 020 (Latchmere House, Ham) was employed as a holding centre after a number of unsatisfactory venues were used. Specially designed for the purpose (it included listening devices in the cells and an absence of visible pipes to prevent Morse communication by prisoners), it was the scene for holding and interrogation of enemy agents. According to the history, 480 internees were taken in during the war, 77 being German, 68 Belgian and 64 French, and the rest a mixture of nationalities (including a number from the Balkans and eastern Europe). Camp WX was formed for longer term holding of prisoners, being located successively at Stafford Prison, the Isle of Man and Dartmoor. The history describes the cells, diet and recreation of those held in some detail, and the various techniques employed during their captivity, including the use of camp agents for the discovery of information. The later sections of the work describe the arrivals on a chronological basis, starting with Waldberg, Meier, Pons and Van der Kieboom in September 1940. Amongst the better known listed for the later stages of the war is the Dutch traitor Christian Lindemanns, also involved in the deception activities in The Netherlands.

KV 4/7 includes reference to the London Reception Centre (LRC) and the interrogation of aliens arriving in Britain during the Second World War. The 'Report on the Operations of the B1D and B1D UK (LRC) in connection with the interrogation of aliens and British subjects arriving in the UK during 1939–1945' contains a history of the LRC and appendices which provide samples of the documentation used at the two centres. A summary of administration and general procedures, record keeping and interrogation methods is included, as well as an indication of the centre's usefulness as a recruiting ground for other organizations, such as the Special Operations Executive and the Secret Intelligence Service. A summary of detentions for 1943–4 is included.

Because of the physical state of these records, many need to be specially produced and seen under supervision.

3.4 Refugees

General policy sources relating to alien refugees may be found in the classes outlined in Section 3.1. In 1941 the responsibility for assessment of grants paid to voluntary organizations dealing with refugees passed from the Home Office to the Assistance Board. The Board was empowered to grant allowances to persons in need as a direct result of war who would not otherwise have been eligible for unemployment assistance. Such persons after 1941 included alien refugees and these wartime function papers may be found in AST 11. General correspondence and papers of the Board are in AST 7.

The Resident Foreigners Section (subsequently Home Division) of the British Council was established in 1940 to look after the interests of the large number of foreigners who came to the UK as refugees from western Europe, as merchant seamen or members of the allied armed forces. The Section organized the teaching of English and supplied books, films, lectures and courses with the two-fold aim of making the refugees feel more at home and so of more use to the war effort and promoting an understanding of the UK which they would disseminate on their return home.

The Section also gave assistance in the running of national and allied centres which were set up in London, Liverpool, and throughout the UK as meeting places for civilians and servicemen of the allied nations. These centres were known as national hearths or houses to make visitors feel they were coming to a home away from home. The centres were administered by the British Council and their records can be found in BW 108: National Hearths: Correspondence and Papers. Only records relating to the London centres are known to have survived. Correspondence includes records relating to Polish, Yugoslavian and Dutch hearths. Files cover the period 1942–6, after which British Council responsibility came to an end.

In addition to general aliens' personal files which include papers relating to refugees (*see* Section 3.2.1), there are also a number of files relating to specific groups of refugees throughout the twentieth century. These are described in the following sections.

3.4.1 Belgian refugees, 1914–19

Shortly after the outbreak of the First World War, Britain was called upon to make provision for very large numbers of homeless refugees from Belgium. The War Refugees Committee established a scheme to remove women and children from the threatened districts of the theatre of war in Europe and place them under conditions of safe keeping in Britain. The total number of refugees from Belgium who came over was upwards of 200,000. A special department was formed at the Local Government Board to deal with all questions relating to war refugees including registration, hospitality, employment, hostels and refuges, transport and repatriation.

The chief refugee camps were in London at the Alexandra Palace Camp, the Earl's Court Refugee Camp, the Edmonton Refuge and Millfield House and these various London refuges provided accommodation for 10,000 refugees between 1914 and repatriation in 1919. The camps were administered internally by the refugees themselves as their facilities included resident medical officers, schools, chapels, playrooms and cinemas.

In October 1914 it was decided that a central register of Belgian refugees should be kept. The resulting register recorded a total of roughly 260,000 names. Valuable information about employment and unemployment among the refugees was also obtained, as well as information about Belgians of military age, which was required by the Belgian military authorities.

Some 2,500 Local Representative Committees were set up throughout the country and many thousands of refugees were maintained locally. Records relating to the work of these communities will be found in local record offices (*see* Appendix 2). Scotland took a prominent part in the reception and care of the refugees. Some 1,500 were sent to Glasgow direct from the port of arrival without passing through the London refuges and many thousands were sent subsequently – the total number of refugees received in Scotland being upwards of 18,000.

The refugees included a considerable number of Jews, especially from Antwerp, who were cared for by the Jewish Society, later the Jewish War Refugees Committee.

Background papers relating to the work undertaken by the British government in the reception and care of Belgian refugees can be found in HO 45 primarily under the subject headings, 'Aliens', 'Nationality', and 'War'. HO 45/10738/261921 provides a useful background history of the Home Office's dealings with Belgian refugees.

The class of records MH 8: War Refugees Committee consists of minutes, history cards, hostel lists, statistics, correspondence and other documents selected for permanent preservation from among the records taken over by the Local Government Board from the voluntary committee which administered relief from public funds to Belgian and other refugees. For Belgian refugees, 1914–19, there is a considerable amount of material entered on the history cards. Each card relates to a whole family, unless the refugee was single with no known relatives. The details given are names, ages, relationships, wife's maiden name, allowances and the address for payment.

Specimen registration forms for Belgian refugees can be found in RG 20/86 and MH 8/6–7.

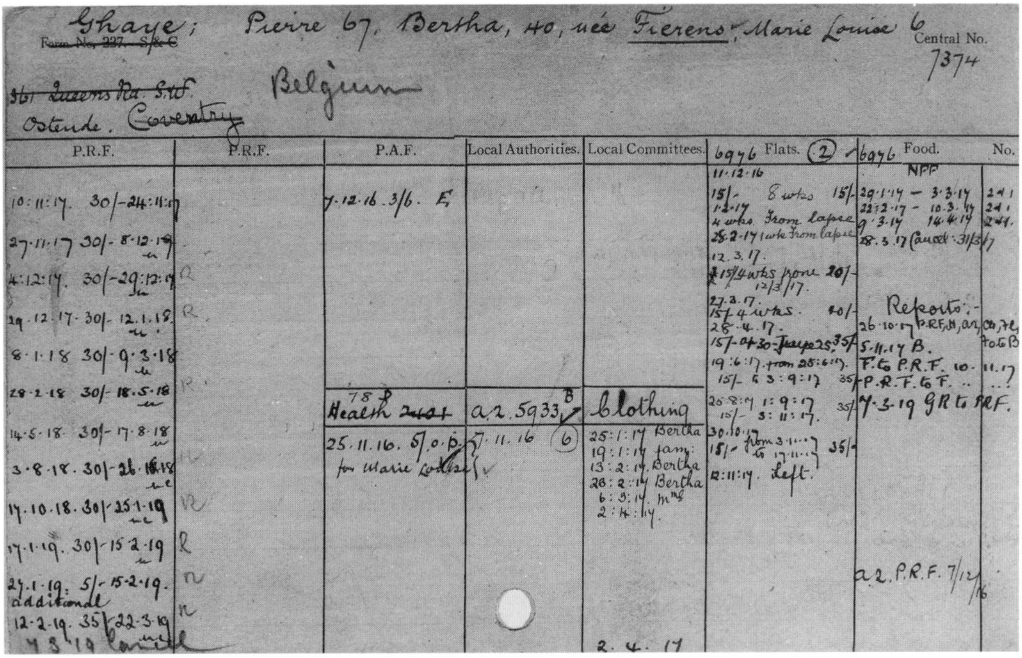

Figure 3 Belgian refugee card for Pierre Ghaye, 1916 (MH 8/58)

3.4.2 Jewish refugees from Nazi Europe

In the 1930s as Jewish refugees began to arrive in the UK from Germany and Austria, it was argued at first that the substantial level of unemployment required a cautious approach. Entry was granted predominantly to those refugees who had the prospect of permanent immigration elsewhere. Camps were set up, such as the Kitchener Camp for Poor Persons in Kent, to house Jewish refugees temporarily pending re-emigration to other countries. Here, over 3,000 Jewish refugees were housed in 1939.

A selection of Home Office files on refugees who did not settle in the UK for the period 1934–48 are in the process of being transferred from the Home Office and these include records relating to Jewish refugees (*see* Section 3.2.1 for further details).

After the *Anschluss* of March 1938, the British government decided to institute a visa system for German and Austrian refugees in order to stem the possible flow that might overwhelm voluntary organizations and create public resentment. With its reluctance to admit a large number of refugees to Britain, the government began to look for suitable centres for settlement within the Empire. The Evian Conference in

July 1938 sought a co-ordinated international solution to the question, but nothing of substance emerged. Many had been admitted to Palestine which had been designated a British mandated territory in 1920, but here the 1937 Peel Commission recommended that no more than 12,000 Jewish immigrants each year should be admitted for fear of Arab reactions to the arrival of Jews.

Jewish records are also held elsewhere. Most of the refugees settled in or around London and the records of the Jewish Temporary Shelter are available at the London Metropolitan Archives (*see* Appendix 2). Other personal files of approximately 400,000 Jewish refugees are still kept by the Jewish Refugees Committee. Further information on Jewish immigrants is available at the Hartley Library at the University of Southampton, and at the Manchester Local Studies Unit. *See* Appendix 4 for the addresses of these archives. Access to them may be restricted.

For earlier Jewish immigrant records, *see* Section 6.2.2 and 8.2.

3.4.3 The Czechoslovak Refugee Trust, 1939–75

The Czechoslovak Refugee Trust was created on 21 July 1939 by deed executed by the Commissioners of HM Treasury, the Home Secretary and three trustees appointed by the Home Secretary. The Trust was wound up in 1975. Records of the Trust are in HO 294: Czechoslovak Refugee Trust Records.

Its original purpose was the assistance of certain categories of people who sought refuge from Nazi persecution following the ceding to Germany of parts of the territory of Czechoslovakia under the Munich Agreement of 30 September 1938, and the dismemberment of Czechoslovakia by the Germans in March 1939. These refugees comprized not only Czechoslovak citizens but several hundred Germans and Austrians who had gained asylum in Czechoslovakia after escaping Nazi persecution in their own countries between 1933 and 1938.

Before the Trust was created, several appeals had been launched in Britain for subscriptions for the relief of the refugees, among them those by the Lord Mayor of London, and the *News Chronicle* and *Manchester Guardian* newspapers. Some of this money was set aside for the use in London for the British Committee for Refugees from Czechoslovakia, a voluntary organization set up in October 1938 to provide temporary hospitality in Britain for especially endangered refugees. British government policy was that the refugees could be accepted in Britain only as transmigrants. Between October 1938 and March 1939 the British Committee brought 3,500 refugees from Czechoslovakia to Britain, which absorbed all the financial resources available to the Committee.

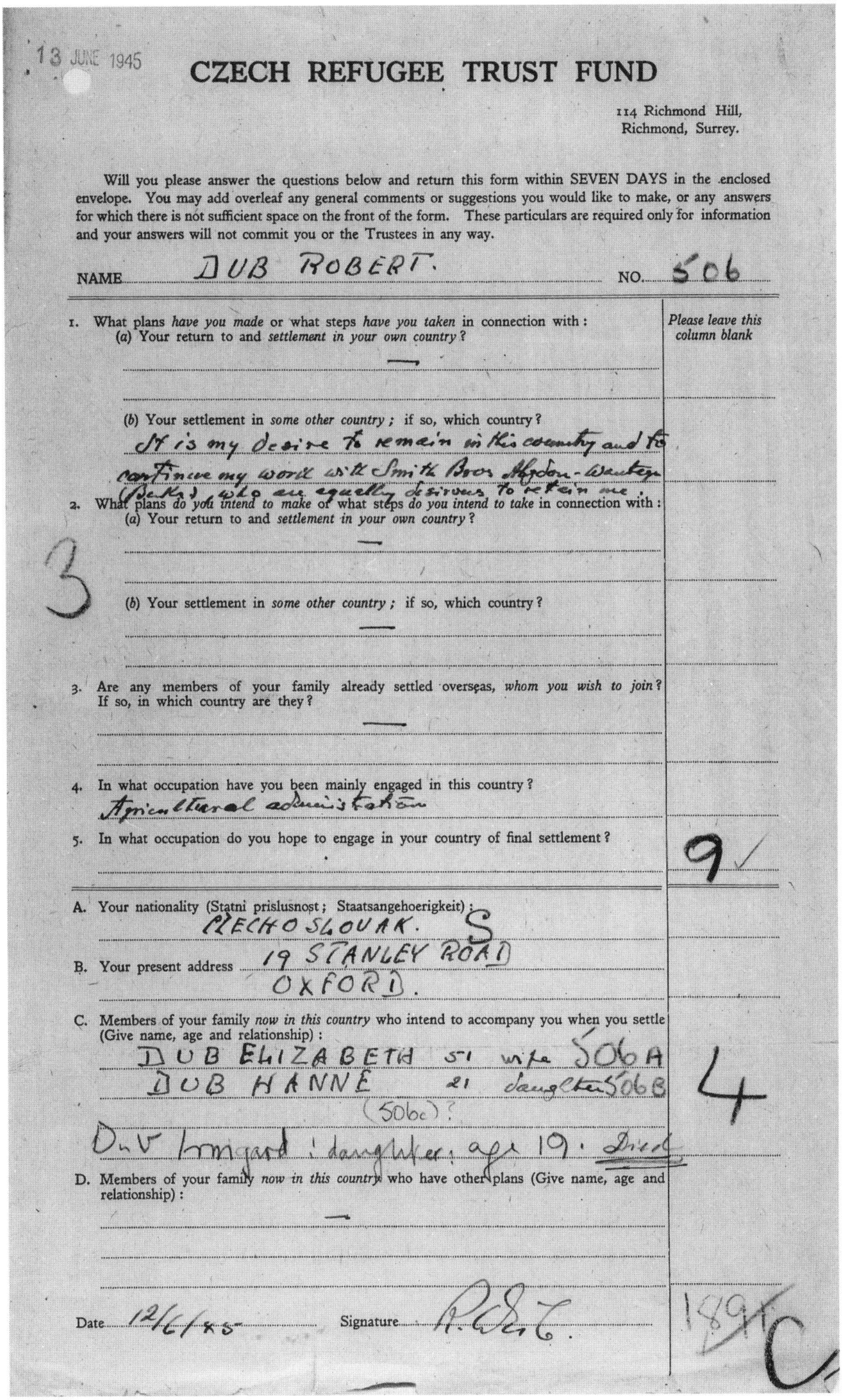

13 JUNE 1945

CZECH REFUGEE TRUST FUND

114 Richmond Hill,
Richmond, Surrey.

Will you please answer the questions below and return this form within SEVEN DAYS in the enclosed envelope. You may add overleaf any general comments or suggestions you would like to make, or any answers for which there is not sufficient space on the front of the form. These particulars are required only for information and your answers will not commit you or the Trustees in any way.

NAME DUB ROBERT. NO. 506

Please leave this column blank

1. What plans *have you made* or what steps *have you taken* in connection with:
   (*a*) Your return to and *settlement in your own country*?
   —
   (*b*) Your settlement in *some other country*; if so, which country?
   It is my desire to remain in this country and to continue my work with Smith Bros Abingdon-Wantage (Berks) who are equally desirous to retain me.
2. What plans *do you intend* to make or what steps *do you intend to take* in connection with:
   (*a*) Your return to and *settlement in your own country*?
   —
   (*b*) Your settlement in *some other country*; if so, which country?
   —
3. Are any members of your family already settled overseas, *whom you wish to join*? If so, in which country are they?
   —
4. In what occupation have you been mainly engaged in this country?
   Agricultural administration
5. In what occupation do you hope to engage in your country of final settlement?

9 ✓

A. Your nationality (Statni prislusnost; Staatsangehoerigkeit): CZECHOSLOVAK. S

B. Your present address 19 STANLEY ROAD OXFORD.

C. Members of your family *now in this country* who intend to accompany you when you settle (Give name, age and relationship):
DUB ELIZABETH 51 wife 506A
DUB HANNE 21 daughter 506B
(506c)?
Dub Irmgard: daughter: age 19. Died

4

D. Members of your family *now in this country* who have other plans (Give name, age and relationship):
—

Date 12/6/45 Signature R. Dub

3

1894 C

Figure 4 Czechoslovak Refugee Trust Fund: questionnaire for Robert Dub, 1945 (HO 294/247)

The method of administering assistance by joint authority of the British and Czechoslovak governments was set out by a treaty dated 27 January 1939 (HO 294/44), subsequently ratified by the Czechoslovakia (Financial Assistance) Act 1939.

In practice the Trust took over where the British Committee left off for want of funds, and when the Czechoslovak government Refugee Department was forced to discontinue operations. The assistance to be afforded to refugees took two forms:

a) emigration to some overseas country of settlement, and
b) maintenance and training in Britain pending re-emigration.

Permanent settlement of refugees was possible on only a very restricted scale during the war, but by the end of 1947 the resettlement of refugees from Nazism had been substantially achieved.

In February 1948 a new category of refugees was created following the coup d'état by which a Communist regime was established in Czechoslovakia, and the British government enlarged the categories of Trust beneficiaries to include refugees from that regime.

The Trust was wound up in 1975 when the Charity Commissioners agreed that the administration of the Fund should pass to the Trustees of the British Council for Aid to Refugees.

HO 294/1–234 are files relating to policy and administration of the fund. Specimen personal files of refugee families in the various categories are in HO 294/235–486. Case papers of other refugee families, extracted from files that have not been preserved, are in HO 294/487–611: in many instances these provide a detailed case history. A numerical index to cases (HO 294/612–13) is open to readers, but the family files and case papers are closed for 50, or occasionally 75, years.

Related files may be found in FO 371, T 210 (Czechoslovak Financial Claims Office: Files), HO 213 and HO 352/139–40. Also, personal files for some of the staff have been selected for HO 382 (Aliens: Personal Files). These records reveal the political and personal conflicts within the organization and are currently being prepared for transfer. In view of the personal information they contain, it is likely that they will be subject to extended closure periods – *see* Section 3.2.1 for further information.

3.4.4 Polish resettlement after the Second World War

Fighting in Europe with the British forces in the Second World War were some 160,000 men of the Polish Army. These soldiers were in the main anti-Communist, and did not want to return to a post-war Poland dominated by the Soviet Union. They were brought back to the UK as a serving unit. The bulk preferred not to be repatriated to Poland and were allowed to stay in the UK. This was organized by the Polish Resettlement Corps, which vetted applicants and discharged them from the Polish armed forces. Wives and dependent relatives of these men were brought to the UK to join them, bringing the total estimated number of cases to over 200,000. For Polish hearth records during the Second World War *see* Section 3.4

3.4.4.1 Polish Resettlement Corps

In order to ease the transition from a Polish military environment to British civilian life, a satisfactory means of demobilization needed to be devised by the British authorities. This took the form of raising, as a corps of the British Army, the Polish Resettlement Corps (PRC), into which Poles were allowed to enlist for the period of their demobilization. The PRC was formed in 1946 and was disbanded after fulfilling its purpose in 1949.

Records of the Corps are in WO 315: Army Records Centre (Polish Section): Polish Records, 1939–50. It should be noted that some of the records are in Polish, although for ease of administration English translations were provided in most cases. The records relate mainly to administrative and policy issues such as organization and disbandment, though WO 315/8 consists of PRC army lists and nominal rolls and WO 315/13–14 are records relating to nursing officers in Polish military hospitals and PRC medical officers, dentists and field ambulance officers.

3.4.4.2 Assistance Board records

The problem of registration, supervision, and settlement of the Poles was a huge one, which imposed a great burden of work not only on the Aliens Branch of the Home Office, but also on all police forces throughout the UK. AST 18: Polish Resettlement contains a selection of files dealing with the problems arising out of the Polish Resettlement Act 1947. The Act placed upon the Assistance Board the responsibility for meeting the needs, either by cash allowance or maintenance in camps or hostels, of certain classes of Poles and their dependants who had come into this country since September 1939. Before then welfare work for Poles had been undertaken by the Polish Wartime Government in exile in London which ceased to function after the British recognized the Polish Government in Warsaw at the end of the war. The work was then temporarily administered by the Interim Treasury Committee for Polish Questions until the Resettlement Act came into force.

The Act enabled the Assistance Board (renamed the National Assistance Board in 1948) to provide accommodation for those whose resettlement was going to take some time to achieve. The Board opened a number of hostels, mainly in the south and south eastern regions of England providing accommodation for over 16,000 Poles. The records in AST 18: Assistance Board and successors: Polish Resettlement, Registered Files (PR Series) reflect the nature of the administrative work of the board and the camps. Related records can be found in AST 7/939, 953, 1053–4, 1063, 1254, 1255, 1456–9, and 1909.

3.4.4.3 Committee for the Education of Poles

The Minister of Education and the Secretary of State for Scotland delegated their powers under Sections 6 and 11 of the Polish Resettlement Act 1947 by setting up on 1 April 1947 the Committee for the Education of Poles in Great Britain. The Committee, an autonomous body consisting of both British and Polish members, had to ensure that the many thousands of Poles who elected to remain in Britain would be fitted for resettlement here or in former British territories overseas. This largely involved acquiring an adequate knowledge of English and of the British way of life. To encourage this the purely Polish institutions maintained by the Committee were eventually dissolved and the children and students educated in equivalent British institutions.

The Committee was wound up on 30 September 1954 with the major part of its task accomplished. The Minister of Education appointed an advisory committee to deal with remaining Polish affairs and a Polish section was established in the Ministry. An Education and Library Committee was also set up at the Polish Research Centre to deal with the Polish libraries and adult education in National Assistance Board Hostels. Both committees were wound up in 1967.

ED 128: Committee for the Education of Poles in Great Britain (Gater Committee), *and* Ministry of Education, Polish Sections of Awards and External Relation Branches: Polish Resettlement Files records the work of the Board (Ministry from 1943) of Education in respect of Polish resettlement. The class includes awards to successful students with questionnaires and life sketches. Previously closed for 75 years, these records (ED 128/42–75) were opened in 1997 following a re-review. The class includes files relating to Polish institutions in Scotland.

3.4.4.4 Welfare Department

LAB 26: Welfare Matters consists of files relating to general welfare matters and includes records relating to housing estates for Polish workers (LAB 26/187–98 and LAB 26/231).

3.4.4.5 Home Office

The majority of aliens arriving between 1940 and 1948 were Poles who eventually applied for naturalization. HO 405 will contain a high proportion of applications from ex-PRC men. For information about the transfer and availability of these records *see* Sections 3.2.1 and 5.4.6.

3.4.5 Hungarian refugees, 1957

In October 1956 Soviet forces entered Hungary following a year that had begun with a gradual and controlled de-Stalinization of policy and escalated into strong attacks on the Communist regime, culminating in mass demonstrations and uprisings among the Hungarian people. The Soviets employed heavy artillery and bombers against the Hungarian freedom fighters. As the frontier with Austria was, by coincidence, physically open for the first time since 1945 and further, for a while, unguarded, a great flood of refugees poured across it. By the end of the year some 153,000 persons had thus sought safety, and many thousands, after being given ready assistance in Austria, found haven in countries in Western Europe and overseas.

A number of case files of Hungarian refugees will appear in the proposed record class, HO 382, though these relate mainly to those who had been here as refugees before 1948. For information about the transfer and accessibility of these records, *see* Section 3.2.1.

HO 352: Aliens, General Matters (ALG Symbol Series) Files relates to general establishment matters, policy and casework of the Aliens Department on a variety of issues relating to aliens and immigration. HO 352/141–9 are files relating to the admission, residence and employment of Hungarian refugees from the Hungarian revolution. Over 21,000 refugees entered the UK between 1957 and 1958, though 6,000 went on to Canada and 1,800 chose to return to Hungary. Files concerning the maintenance of Hungarian refugees can be found in AST 7/1621–3. LAB 8/2344 and LAB 8/2371 detail Ministry of Labour administrative and employment arrangements for Hungarian refugees.

3.5 Internees

During the First and Second World Wars enemy aliens were interned by the British authorities. In both wars internment camps were established within the United Kingdom. Many internee records are held in local archives – *see* Appendix 2.

3.5.1 First World War

Very few records of individual internees survive for the First World War. Lists of names of internees were routinely forwarded to the Prisoners of War Information

Bureau in London, which in turn informed the International Red Cross Headquarters in Geneva. The lists compiled by the Bureau were largely destroyed by bombing in 1940. However, two specimen lists of German subjects interned as POWs in 1915–16 can be found in WO 900/45 and 46. The list is divided into army, naval and civilian prisoners, and gives the regiment, ship or home address of each prisoner.

A classified list of interned enemy aliens can be found in HO 144/11720/364868. Nominal rolls of male enemy aliens of the age of 45 and upwards, submitted to the Secretary of State by commandants of internment camps, are included among a census of aliens in the United Kingdom from 1915 to 1924 in HO 45/11522/287235. Lists of alien enemies detained in Lunatic Asylums within the Metropolitan Police District can also be found in this document.

Among the older papers attached to some of the files in the proposed classes HO 382 and HO 405 are First World War appeals against internment. For information relating to the transfer and accessibility of these records, *see* Section 3.2.1.

References to individual internees can also be found in the card index to the Foreign Office general correspondence in the Research Enquiries Room. Any reference found on a card needs to be turned into a modern PRO reference: for guidance on doing this, *see* Overseas Records Information leaflets 12 and 13. It should be noted that the presence of a card does not necessarily mean that the papers to which it relates have survived

Home Office records dealing primarily with policy relating to internees and internment camps can be found in HO 45 and HO 144. Both classes of records are arranged by subject matter and papers relating to internment and internees may be found under the headings 'Aliens', 'Nationality', and 'War'.

Other material on internees is in correspondence of the Metropolitan Police in MEPO 2. This includes MEPO 2/1633 which consists of the administration of Islington Internment Camp during the First World War.

3.5.2 Second World War: policy

Internees were primarily enemy aliens, but during the first two years of the Second World War other aliens were also interned, including many refugees who had fled Nazi Germany to escape persecution. Fears of invasion led to a general feeling of hostility towards all enemy aliens. After the outbreak of war in September 1939, known Nazi sympathizers were rounded up. This was the start of a campaign which lasted until mid-1940, by which time 8,000 internees had been gathered into camps, to be deported to the dominions. This harsh policy was gradually relaxed after the sinking of the SS *Arandora Star* by a German U-boat in July 1940, with the loss of 800

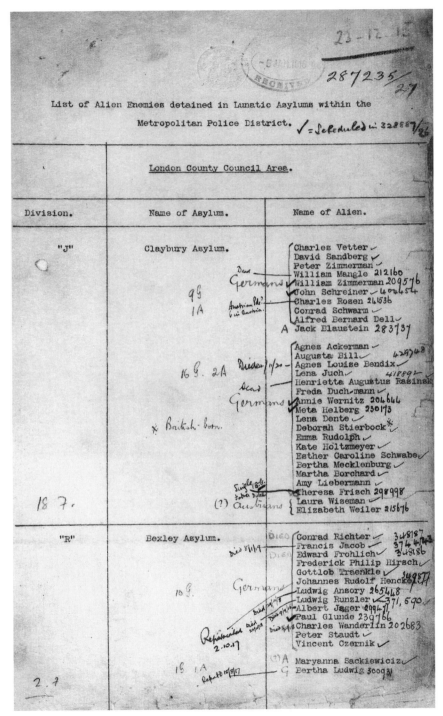

Figure 5 List of aliens detained in lunatic asylums within the Metropolitan Police District, 1915 (HO 45/11522/287235)

internees. This disaster led to vigorous protests about the British internment policy, which was changed so that enemy aliens were interned in camps in Britain.

Most internees had been released by the end of 1942. Of those that remained, many were repatriated from 1943 onwards. It was not, however, until late 1945 that the last internees were released.

3.5.3 Second World War: personal records

A small sample of 75 personal case files of internees survive for the Second World War. These records can be found in the class of records HO 214: Internees: Personal Files and are particularly useful in depicting the life of an internee. The files were created whenever the Home Office became involved in a personal case for whatever reason. Some personal files for aliens whose internee personal files survive in HO 214 are gradually being transferred to the PRO from the Home Office. These records will be available in the classes HO 382 and HO 405. For information relating to the transfer and accessibility of these records, *see* Section 3.2.1.

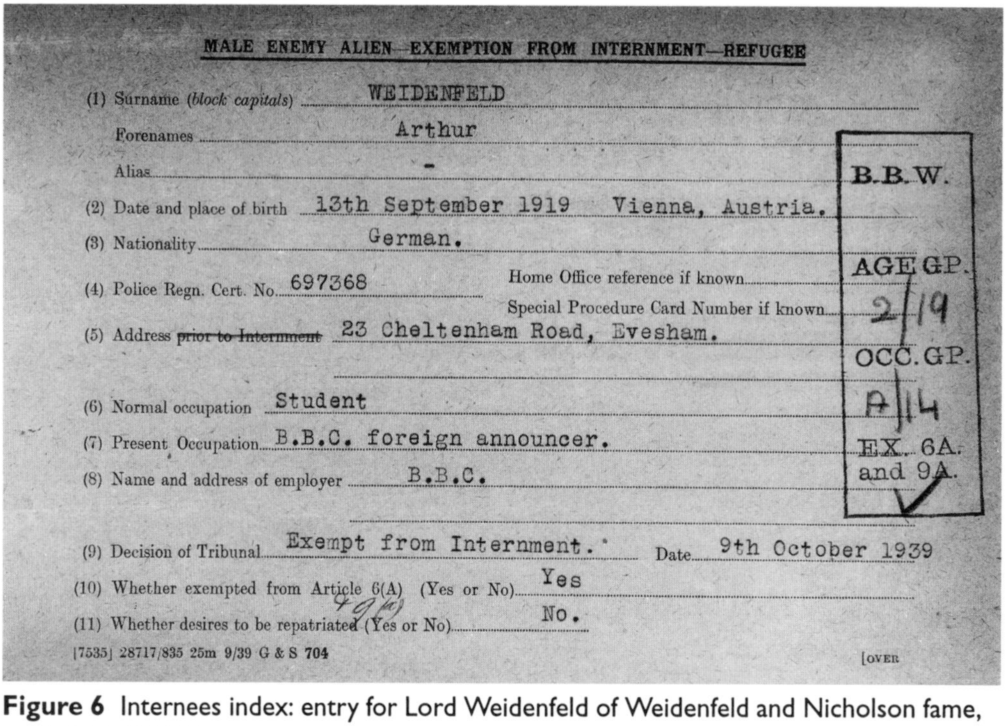
MALE ENEMY ALIEN—EXEMPTION FROM INTERNMENT—REFUGEE

(1) Surname (*block capitals*) WEIDENFELD
Forenames Arthur
Alias -
(2) Date and place of birth 13th September 1919 Vienna, Austria.
(3) Nationality German.
(4) Police Regn. Cert. No. 697368 Home Office reference if known
Special Procedure Card Number if known
(5) Address ~~prior to Internment~~ 23 Cheltenham Road, Evesham.
(6) Normal occupation Student
(7) Present Occupation B.B.C. foreign announcer.
(8) Name and address of employer B.B.C.
(9) Decision of Tribunal Exempt from Internment. Date 9th October 1939
(10) Whether exempted from Article 6(A) (Yes or No) Yes
(11) Whether desires to be repatriated (Yes or No) No.

B.B.W.
AGE GP. 2/19
OCC. GP. A/14
EX. 6A. and 9A.

[7535] 28717/835 25m 9/39 G & S 704 [OVER

Figure 6 Internees index: entry for Lord Weidenfeld of Weidenfeld and Nicholson fame, 1939 (HO 396/98)

HO 396: Aliens Department: Internees Index consists of 307 sets of records which give details of mostly Germans, Austrians and Italians and their spouses who were interned or considered for internment by internment tribunals. The slips, which date from 1939 to 1947, are available on microfilm in the Microfilm Reading Room. The records are usually grouped by nationality, and are in alphabetical order within each set. The slips within these binders give personal information on the front and sometimes details of the individual's case on the reverse side. Details usually include date of birth, address, occupation and details of employers. Slips concerning aliens who were considered by internment tribunals to be exempt from internment are open without restriction. Only the front of slips where a decision was made to intern an individual are open without restriction. If researchers wish to have access to information recorded on the reverse side, they can write to the Departmental Record Officer of the Home Office (*see* Appendix 4 for address), who may send a photocopy if the information can be released.

References to individual internees and internment camps may be found in the printed indexes of the general correspondence of the Foreign Office, available in the Research Enquiries Room. Any reference found in the index needs to be turned into a modern PRO reference. It should be noted that the presence of an index entry does not necessarily mean that the papers to which it relates have survived. A 'How to Use' leaflet concerning these indexes is available on request at the Research Enquiries Desk.

Other Foreign Office records relating to enemy aliens interned by the British, are in FO 916. The class consists of general files relating to reports on internment camps and a number of lists of alien internees, arranged by location, name and number of camp.

Information about enemy aliens and internees in the colonies can be found in CO 968 (some records, however, are subject to extended closure).

For references to deported internees *see* Section 3.7.2.

3.5.4 Second World War: camps

Nominal camp lists of internees can be found in HO 215: Internment: General Files. These records are arranged by name of internment camp and the documents record the internee's name, date of birth and (if applicable) date of release. In addition, the Home Office Internment (General) Files in HO 215 contain a large amount of material on Home Office involvement with the internment of enemy aliens and prisoners of war (POWs) and includes correspondence between the Home Office and the (UK) Prisoners of War Information Bureau (PWIB). The class contains general files relating to internment during the Second World War including subjects such as conditions in camps, visits to camps, classification and segregation of internees, regulations and enactments, and the movement of internees abroad.

HO 213: Aliens Department: General (GEN) Files and Aliens Naturalization and Nationality (ALN and NTY Symbol Series) Files also contains a selection of files relating to internment camps during the Second World War. For example, correspondence concerning the treatment of interned enemy aliens is in HO 213/494–8. Further information may also be found in the classes HO 45 and HO 144 under the subject headings 'Aliens', 'Nationality' and 'War'.

See also Section 3.3.

3.6 Prisoners of war

During the First and Second World Wars captured enemy armed forces personnel were imprisoned. In both wars prisoner of war camps were established within the United Kingdom. Many prisoner of war records are held in local archives – *see* Appendix 2.

3.6.1 First World War

Very few records of individual enemy prisoners of war survive for the First World War. Lists of names of enemy prisoners were routinely forwarded to the Prisoners of War Information Bureau in London, which in turn informed the International Red Cross Headquarters in Geneva. The lists compiled by the Bureau were largely destroyed by bombing in 1940. However, two specimen lists of German subjects interned as POWs in 1915–16 can be found in WO 900/45 and 46. The list is divided into army, naval and civilian prisoners, and gives the regiment, ship or home address of each prisoner.

Correspondence about enemy merchant seamen taken prisoner is in MT 9 code 106. Files concerning the employment of enemy POWs in Britain are among the records of the Ministry of National Service (Labour Supply Department), and can be found in NATS 1/567–71.

A substantial amount of material relating to POWs (British, allied and enemy) is contained in the General Political Correspondence of the Foreign Office in FO 371. References can be found in the Foreign Office General Correspondence (1906–19) card index, which is located in the Reference Room. In addition, FO 566/1837–74 contains 'Prisoners and Aliens Registers, 1915–1919', arranged by country. A large proportion of this correspondence has not survived.

The International Council of the Red Cross in Geneva keeps list of all known POWs and internees of all nationalities for both the First and Second World Wars. Searches are only made in response to written requests and an hourly search fee is charged. *See* Appendix 4 for the address.

3.6.2 Second World War: policy

The War Office was responsible for the custody of POWs of all services. The war diaries of the Directorate of Prisoners of War are in WO 165/59–71, and minutes and reports of the Imperial Prisoners of War Committee meetings can also be found there. Some selected war diaries of hospitals, depots and camps are in WO 177/1833–55. and selected diaries of POW camps can be found in WO 166; there is a general index at the beginning of this class.

Correspondence with the United States authorities on policy concerning POWs in general can be found among the papers of the British Joint Staff Mission in Washington (CAB 122). The Operational Papers of the Prime Minister's Office (PREM 3/363 and 364) contain material relating to both enemy and allied POWs. Correspondence between the British government, the Red Cross and the Protecting Powers, including inspection reports on POW camps, is among the records of the Consular (War) Department of the Foreign Office, in FO 916. The few surviving records of the Prisoners of War Information Bureau itself are in WO 307. CO 968/33–6 contain correspondence of the Colonial Office Defence section relating to internment policy in the British colonies, and include lists of enemy POWs in various colonial territories. Correspondence about the employment of Italian merchant seamen taken prisoner is in MT 9 code 106.

The Prisoners of War and Internees Files in the Admiralty and Secretariat Papers (ADM 1 code 79) contain documentation on many aspects of the Royal Navy's involvement with the capture and internment of enemy and allied POWs, naval and other services. Similar correspondence and papers are to be found in the Prisoners of War and Internees Files in the Admiralty and Secretariat Cases (ADM 116 code 79). Many of these files contain lists of Royal Navy personnel interned in enemy camps, although they are not identifiable from the class lists.

3.6.3 Second World War: personal records

Registered Papers concerning prisoners both during and after the Second World War are in WO 32 code 91. The Medical Historian's Papers in WO 222 include reports on the health of POWs and on the work of POW hospitals. The War Diary of MI19, the division of Military Intelligence responsible for the interrogation of enemy POWs, is in WO 165/41. Records of the Combined Services Detailed Interrogation Centre (CSDIC) and of the Prisoners of War Interrogation Section can be found in WO 208. Many of these files are closed for 75 years, although the CSDIC reports in WO 208/4117–4212 are now open. A few interrogation reports made on German POWs in 1944 exist in the files of the Control Commission for Germany: Internal Affairs and Communications Division, in FO 1050/169. Interrogation reports on enemy airmen among the records of the Air Ministry's Directorate of Intelligence (AIR 40) are closed for 75 years. Some debriefings of enemy POWs can be found in the files concerning the Prisoners of War Campaign conducted by the Political Warfare Executive of the Foreign Office, in FO 898/320–30.

The International Council of the Red Cross in Geneva (for address *see* Appendix 4) keeps lists of all known POWs and internees of all nationalities for both the First and Second World Wars. For further information, *see* Section 3.6.1.

3.6.4 Second World War: camps

War diaries of units of the British Army contain material on POW camps, labour companies, etc. in various theatres of war. These can in most cases be identified from the indexes to the appropriate class lists. Numerous files on individual POW camps in the United Kingdom are among the records of the Prisoners of War Section of the London-based Control Office for Germany and Austria (FO 939). Lists of POW and internment camps are among the Military Headquarters Papers: Home Forces, in WO 199/404–409. Nominal lists of enemy POWs temporarily interned in the Tower of London can be found in WO 94/105.

3.6.5 Former prisoners of war, 1945

With the termination of hostilities in Europe in May 1945 not all POWs wanted to be repatriated from the UK. Normally, POWs are, on the conclusion of hostilities, returned to their homeland. It was found that many of the 'German' POWs in the UK were not in fact German nationals but people of various central European origins who had been pressed into service with the Nazi war machine. Legally, they could have been returned to Germany, but in many cases it was found almost impossible to enforce such removal, since doing so would have resulted in the men concerned becoming displaced persons (DPs) in Germany. The option was therefore given to certain POWs, who were captured in German uniform, to remain in the UK and almost 20,000 men availed themselves of this concession. The selected men were released from POW status and placed on conditions which tied them to agricultural duties.

The majority of the records outlined below were generated by the Control Commission for Germany and its predecessors. Allied authority in Germany was exercised between 1945 and 1949 by the commanders-in-chief of the various allied military zones, and jointly through a control council. In 1949, that authority was transferred from the military governors to civil high commissioners. In London, the department responsible for the exercising of British control in Germany and Austria was the Control Office, which in 1947 became the German Section of the Foreign Office.

Documentation on all aspects of the work of the Control Office's Prisoner of War Section may be found in FO 939. This class includes files on individual POW camps in the United Kingdom. The records of the Control Office's General Department, in FO 945, contain files on the repatriation of ex-POWs (mainly Austrian and German) in FO 945/441–59. Files of the Displaced Persons Section are to be found in FO 945/359–404, 544–773, and material on the resettlement of DPs exists in FO 945/460–527. The financial aspects of DP administration in Austria and Germany are documented in the Control Office Finance files in FO 944. Information on travel into and out of Germany by ex-POWs and DPs holding Ministry of Labour permits is in the Control Office Travel files in FO 940.

LAB 26: Welfare Matters consists of files relating to general welfare matters and includes records relating to the recruitment of DPs for work in Britain (LAB 26/230). Other related files may be found among the general sources referred to in Section 3.1.

3.7 Deportees

The power to expel aliens who had become paupers or criminals was first given under the Aliens Act 1905 and continued under subsequent amendments to the Act and an Order in Council made in 1920.

Courts could recommend the deportation of an alien found guilty of certain specified crimes or of an offence for which a fine could not be substituted for imprisonment. Deportation could be recommended in addition to or in lieu of sentence. The Home Secretary was not bound to act on the recommendation of the court and might decide not to make an expulsion order, for example in cases where a person had been resident for a long time or might suffer political persecution on return to the native country. The Home Secretary could also deport an alien who had not committed a criminal offence if it appeared to be in the public interest. Common reasons for such expulsions were failure to register with or report regularly to the police, ignoring work restrictions, and becoming a charge on public funds. Deported aliens were not permitted to return.

3.7.1 General sources

The registers of deportees in HO 372 date from 1906 until 1963 and are mostly large pre-printed volumes completed in manuscript. The information given is usually name, nationality, date of conviction, offence, whether or not the deportation order was revoked

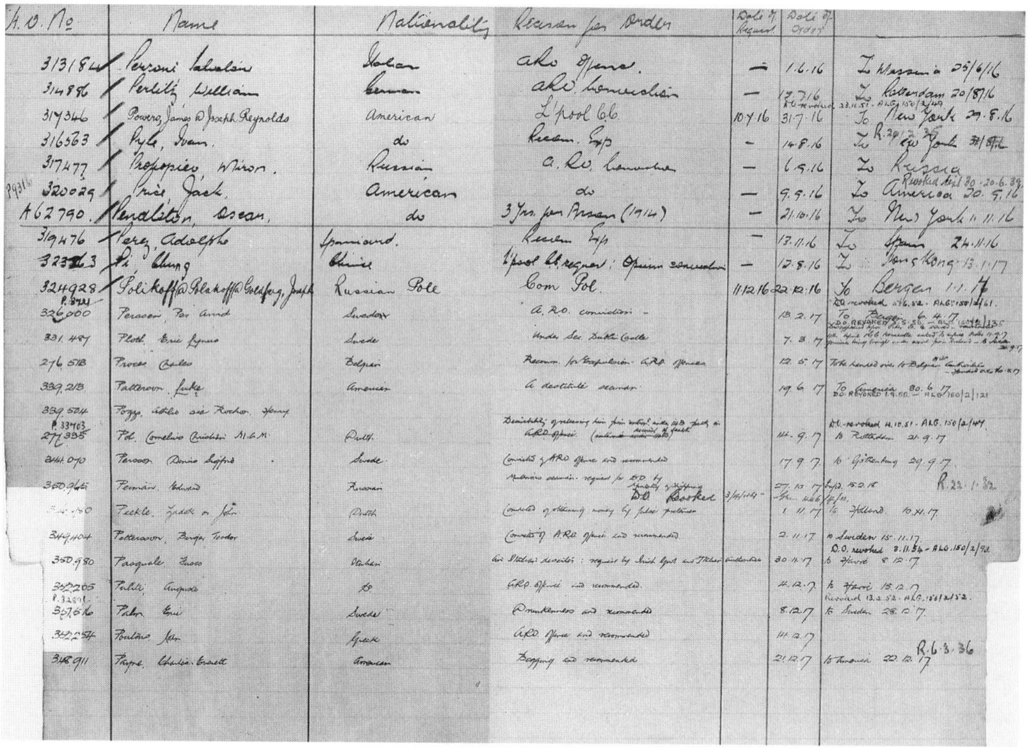

Figure 7 Register of deportation orders, 1916 (HO 372/19)

and, if so, when. The volumes are arranged chronologically. The order authorizing an individual's deportation was filed on the alien's personal file (*see* Section 3.2.1).

Other sources for deportees include HO 45 and HO 144 under the subject headings 'Aliens', 'Nationality', and 'War'. Although most of these files deal mainly with policy and administrative matters, some relate to specific deportation cases.

The PRO does not hold the records of the courts of summary jurisdiction which for England and Wales were the Petty, Borough and Quarter Sessions, and magistrates courts. Instead, these are held in local county archives (*see* Appendix 2). As Scotland has always had a separate legal system, the relevant Scottish records, including those of courts of summary jurisdiction, are held in Scotland.

3.7.2 Second World War: deportations

For the first two years of the Second World War, approximately 8,000 enemy aliens were temporarily interned in British camps prior to being deported to the colonies and the dominions. Passenger lists survive for merchant vessels leaving British ports for ports outside Europe and the Mediterranean Sea in BT 27: Outwards Passenger Lists. These records are arranged by date and port of departure and are not indexed by surname. In order to use them it is necessary to know the name of the ship and preferably port of departure in order to avoid a very time consuming and speculative search. Registers of passenger lists in BT 32 give, under the different ports, the names of ships and the months of departure. These records are available on open access in the Research Enquiries Room. For further information on passenger lists, *see* Section 4.2.

Many ships carrying deported internees were lost at sea by enemy action and these losses resulted in the ending of the policy of deporting internees. BT 334: Registrar General of Shipping and Seamen: Registers and indexes of births, marriages and deaths of passengers and seamen at sea, includes returns for aliens. Related records may also be found in HO 213, HO 214 and HO 215. Survivors' reports from lost vessels can be found among the Admiralty war history cases and papers in ADM 1, ADM 116 and ADM 199. A card index, arranged by name of vessel, is located in the Research Enquiries Room. Similarly, official inquiries into such losses may be found among the War Cabinet Memoranda in CAB 66.

4 Certificates of arrival and passenger lists

4.1 Certificates of arrival

4.1.1 1793–1815

A system of aliens' control was introduced as a wartime measure by an Act (33 Geo. III, c. IV) passed in 1793 'for establishing regulations respecting Aliens arriving in this Kingdom, or resident therein, in certain cases'. This Act was extended by subsequent Acts until the end of the Napoleonic Wars. The Aliens Acts 1793 and 1798 established a system of registration of aliens by means of declarations signed by aliens at ports of entry and certified into the Home Office by customs officers or local agents. Resident aliens and those arriving in Great Britain after January 1793 had to give their names, ranks, occupations and addresses to a local Justice of the Peace (JP). The Home Secretary sent round a circular in March 1797 asking for details of those who had arrived since May 1792. Householders who took in an alien as a lodger had to deliver similar details to the overseer of the parish and returns and samples of these 'Accounts of Aliens' and 'Householders' Notices and Overseers' Returns' were sent to the Clerk of the Peace so that he could lay them before Quarter Sessions. Such lists may be found among returns of Quarter Sessions at county archives (see Appendix 2). For example, there are 38 accounts of aliens from eight Middlesex parishes in 1797 and 10 householders' notices from five parishes in 1798 included in Quarter Session records at the London Metropolitan Archives.

Aliens had to secure passports from the Secretary of State in order to leave London, and were restricted to certain ports of entry and to certain areas of residence inland. In 1793 a superintendent of aliens was appointed, and his department became known as the Aliens Office which was accommodated in the Home Office until 1798. It was concerned with the registration of aliens and issued directions to local agents, mayors and local officials on the detention or expulsion of aliens, and made enquiries about the character of foreigners seeking naturalization.

Most of the early records of the Aliens Office have been destroyed but FO 83/21–2 contains lists of aliens arriving at British ports for the period August 1810 – May 1811.

4.1.2 1816–25

The wartime regulations and powers regarding aliens were repealed at the peace of 1814, but were renewed with modifications later in the same year and again in 1815. In 1816 an Act was passed (56 Geo. III c. 86). The Act required masters of vessels to declare in writing to the Inspector of Aliens or Officer of the Customs the number of aliens on board, specifying their names and descriptions, and the aliens themselves were required to make a similar declaration. Each alien was to be issued on arrival with a certificate, showing the ship's name, and his or her own name, description, place of departure, destination, and profession, with space for references and remarks. Unless he or she was a servant, the alien was to produce the certificate within one week to a magistrate or a JP, and copies of the entries on the certificates were to be sent both by the port and by the magistrate or JP to the Secretary of State in London. The Act applied to all aliens except seamen, ambassadors and their domestic servants, and children under 14. Most of these provisions had previously been included in the 1793 Act but this Act made the first provision for any central system of registration. It was, however, confined to aliens arriving in the country from abroad and did not apply to those already here.

No certificates of arrival of aliens survive for this period.

4.1.3 1826–1905

The Act was continued until 1826, when there was passed a new 'Act for the Registration of Aliens' (7 Geo. IV c. 46). This contained a requirement that from 1 July 1826 every alien should make a declaration 'of his name, abode, etc.; and transmit the same within fourteen days to the Aliens Office in Great Britain, or to the chief secretary for Ireland'. Aliens were thereafter required to send to the Secretary of State, or to the Chief Secretary for Ireland, a declaration of their place of residence every six months, and the clerk at the Aliens Office was to send in return a certificate similar to that described in the 1816 Act. The requirements of the 1793 and 1816 Acts regarding the declaration to be made by masters of vessels and by aliens on arrival were retained, together with the requirement that aliens arriving in this country should be given certificates and copies sent to the Secretary of State. Aliens were no longer required to produce their certificates to a magistrate or JP, but they were to produce them at the Aliens Office if residing within five miles of the City of Westminster, or to make a declaration in writing if they lived further away. They were also required to make a declaration before leaving the country, and, for the first time, they were required to produce police registration certificates. Like the 1816 Act, this Act did not apply to seamen, ambassadors and their domestic servants, or children under 14, and a new provision was included to the effect that aliens should also be exempt who had been continually residing in the country for at least seven years, provided they held a certificate to this effect from the Aliens Office. This Act remained in force until 1836.

A new Act (7 Will. IV c. II) was passed in 1836 and repealed the Act of 1826; it introduced some relaxation in the system of registration but continued the requirement that masters of vessels and aliens should make a declaration on arrival. Aliens were still given a certificate, and copies of the certificates were sent to the Secretary of State in London. Aliens were still required to produce police registration certificates but it was no longer necessary for them to visit or send a written declaration to the Aliens Office, and the declaration they made on leaving the country was in future to be made at the Customs Office at the port of departure. An alien living in this country was no longer required to report his or her address every six months, and was in future to become exempt from the provisions of the Act after three years instead of seven.

This Act remained in force until it was repealed by the Aliens Act 1905. The provisions of the 1816, 1826 and 1836 Acts were directed mainly against foreign 'criminal and hostile persons' and they were concerned with maintaining a check on aliens entering or already in the country rather than with excluding them at the ports. It was not until the end of the nineteenth century that any concern was felt at the likely effect of alien immigration on the employment situation of British workers and it was not until 1905 that any provision was made to deal with it: *see* Chapter 3.

Certificates issued under the Aliens Act 1826 were destroyed when the Aliens Office was absorbed into the Home Office in 1836, but there is an index of certificates from 1826 to 1849 in HO 5/25–32. HO 2 contains original certificates of arrival of individual aliens arranged under ports of arrival for the period 1836–52. Each certificate gives the alien's name, nationality, profession, date of arrival and last country visited, with a signature, and occasionally other particulars. The Treasury agreed to a proposal in 1849 by Sir George Grey, the Secretary of State for the Home Department, to abolish the register and no certificates survive after 1852. An alphabetical unpublished index of alien certificates of some German, Polish and Prussian persons, 1847–52, compiled by the Anglo-German Family History Society, is available in the Research Enquiries Room. *See* Appendix 4 for the address of this society.

HO 3 consists of returns of alien passengers made by masters of ships under s.2 of the Act of 1836. The lists survive for the period July 1836 to December 1869 but no lists survive for the period January 1861 to December 1866. After 1869 the Home Office preserved the lists for only five years after which they were destroyed. The lists are arranged chronologically and there are four per year. There are no name indexes though the Anglo-German Family History Society have extracted some 36,000 names from the period 1853–69. It is also worth noting that, as the declarations are usually made by ship's captains, it is often difficult to decipher the information supplied.

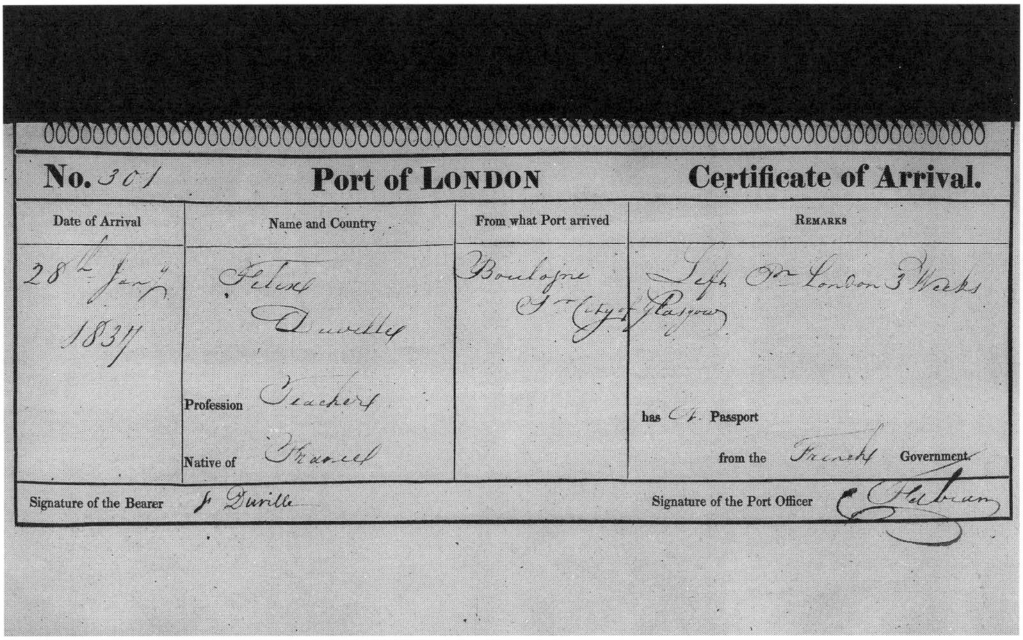

No. 301 Port of LONDON Certificate of Arrival.

Date of Arrival	Name and Country	From what Port arrived	REMARKS
28th Jany 1837	Felix Duville Profession Teacher Native of France	Boulogne	has a Passport from the French Government

Signature of the Bearer F Duville Signature of the Port Officer

Figure 8 Certificate of arrival (no. 301) for Felix Duville, a teacher from France. He arrived in London from Boulogne, January 1837 (HO 2/21)

In the minutes of evidence taken before the Select Committee on Laws affecting Aliens in 1843 (Parliamentary Papers reference 1843, volume V, page 145), it was reported that at Liverpool in 1842 no lists were provided by the masters and there was no registration of aliens; at other ports the masters' lists showed that many aliens landed but failed to register. At London, 7,716 landed and 4,493 registered; at Dover, 1,277 landed and 1,237 registered; at Southampton, 1,197 landed and none registered; at Hull, 794 landed and one registered. In all, 11,600 aliens landed and 6,084 registered. In theory, the penalty for an alien failing to register was £2, and for a master failing to provide a list £20, but it appears that these fines were never exacted.

4.1.4 Other records

HO 5 includes out-letters and entry books of the Home Office and the Aliens Office relating to aliens and registers of applications for denization. The class covers the period 1794 to 1921, though between 1871 and 1873, such out-letters will be found in HO 136. These records include Home Office correspondence concerning a variety of issues relating to aliens during this period and the pieces often include a nominal index.

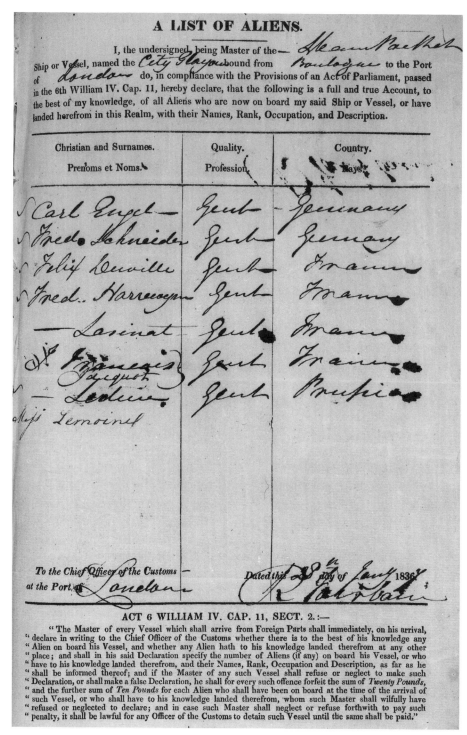

Figure 9 List of aliens, including Felix Duville from France, January 1837 (HO 3/3)

4.2 Board of Trade passenger lists

The Merchant Shipping Act 1894 (57 & 58 Vict. c. 60) required the listing of passengers on board British merchant vessels. Ships' passenger lists among the records of the Board of Trade relate mainly to arrivals in and departures from UK seaports. The lists were deposited with the Board of Trade by the various passenger ship lines. They are arranged in two series, BT 26: Arrivals and BT 27: Departures.

To find a document you should know the port of departure/arrival and the date. Some ports are not named separately, but included with other ports nearby; see the explanatory note at the front of the BT 26 and BT 27 class lists for details. Some ports are also known by different names, e.g. Queenstown might be entered as Cork. If you do not know the port of arrival/departure, but do know the name of the ship, you could consult the Registers of Passenger Lists, 1906–51, in BT 32 – *see* Section 4.2.3. If you do not know port of arrival or departure or name of ship, it will be very difficult and time consuming to find any record.

Many passenger lists are in a fragile condition, and searching them can be very time consuming. There are no indexes of names, and most lists are not alphabetical. The information given varies, but can include age, occupation, and sometimes a proposed address in the UK. There are separate lists for British passengers and alien passengers. The lists are arranged monthly by port of arrival or departure. To use them you need to know at least the approximate date of arrival or departure and the port, if you are to have any realistic hope of finding a passenger's name. These records are produced in the Map and Large Document Room.

Copies of passenger lists can sometimes be found at shipping archives, such as P&O archives (*see* Appendix 4 for address).

4.2.1 Arrivals, 1878–1960

BT 26 contains the 'Passenger Lists, Inwards', 1878–88 and 1890–1960. These give the names of all passengers arriving in the UK, where the ship's voyage began at a port outside Europe and the Mediterranean Sea. Names of passengers who boarded these ships at European ports and disembarked in the UK will be included. However, note that passenger lists for ships whose voyages both began and ended within Europe are not included. For example, no lists survive for voyages between the UK and Ireland.

There is a small collection only of lists between 1878 and 1888. The continuous run begins in 1890.

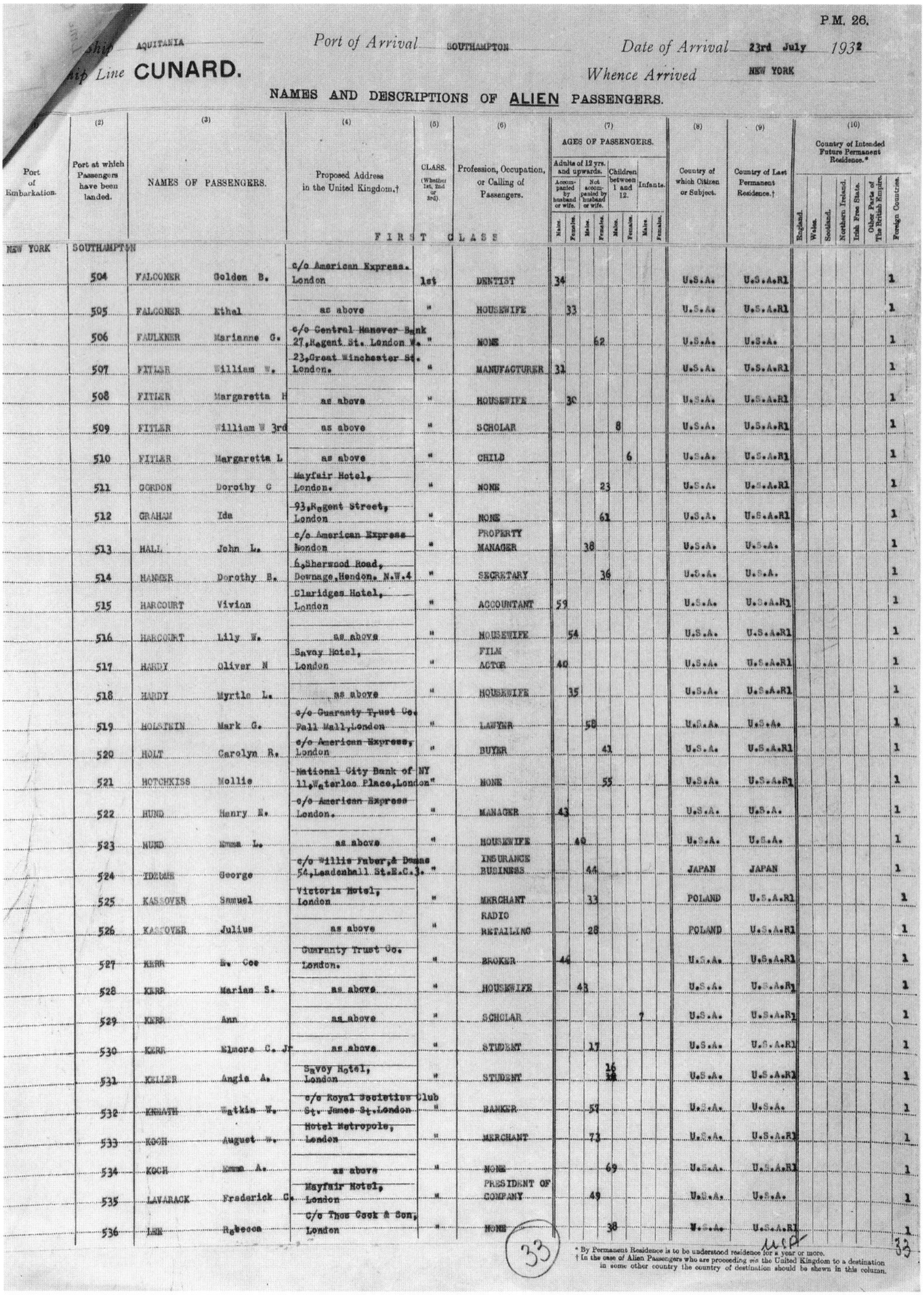

P.M. 26.

Ship AQUITANIA Port of Arrival SOUTHAMPTON Date of Arrival 23rd July 1932

Ship Line CUNARD. Whence Arrived NEW YORK

NAMES AND DESCRIPTIONS OF ALIEN PASSENGERS.

(1) Port of Embarkation.	(2) Port at which Passengers have been landed.	(3) NAMES OF PASSENGERS.	(4) Proposed Address in the United Kingdom.†	(5) CLASS. (Whether 1st, 2nd or 3rd).	(6) Profession, Occupation, or Calling of Passengers.	(7) AGES OF PASSENGERS. Adults of 12 yrs. and upwards. Accompanied by husband or wife. Males.	Females.	Not accompanied by husband or wife. Males.	Females.	Children between 1 and 12. Males.	Females.	Infants. Males.	Females.	(8) Country of which Citizen or Subject.	(9) Country of Last Permanent Residence.†	(10) Country of Intended Future Permanent Residence.* England.	Wales.	Scotland.	Northern Ireland.	Irish Free State.	Other Parts of The British Empire.	Foreign Countries.
				FIRST CLASS																		
NEW YORK	SOUTHAMPTON																					
	504	FALCONER Golden B.	c/o American Express. London	1st	DENTIST	34								U.S.A.	U.S.A.R1							1
	505	FALCONER Ethel	as above	"	HOUSEWIFE		33							U.S.A.	U.S.A.R1							1
	506	FAULKNER Marianne G.	c/o Central Hanover Bank 27, Regent St. London W.	"	NONE				62					U.S.A.	U.S.A.							1
	507	FITLER William W.	23, Great Winchester St. London.	"	MANUFACTURER	31								U.S.A.	U.S.A.R1							1
	508	FITLER Margaretta H	as above	"	HOUSEWIFE		30							U.S.A.	U.S.A.R1							1
	509	FITLER William W 3rd	as above	"	SCHOLAR					8				U.S.A.	U.S.A.R1							1
	510	FITLER Margaretta L	as above	"	CHILD						6			U.S.A.	U.S.A.R1							1
	511	GORDON Dorothy C	Mayfair Hotel, London.	"	NONE				23					U.S.A.	U.S.A.R1							1
	512	GRAHAM Ida	93, Regent Street, London	"	NONE				61					U.S.A.	U.S.A.R1							1
	513	HALL John L.	c/o American Express London	"	PROPERTY MANAGER			38						U.S.A.	U.S.A.							1
	514	HAMMER Dorothy B.	6, Sherwood Road, Downage, Hendon. N.W.4	"	SECRETARY				36					U.S.A.	U.S.A.							1
	515	HARCOURT Vivian	Claridges Hotel, London	"	ACCOUNTANT	59								U.S.A.	U.S.A.R1							1
	516	HARCOURT Lily W.	as above	"	HOUSEWIFE		54							U.S.A.	U.S.A.R1							1
	517	HARDY Oliver N	Savoy Hotel, London	"	FILM ACTOR	40								U.S.A.	U.S.A.R1							1
	518	HARDY Myrtle L.	as above	"	HOUSEWIFE		35							U.S.A.	U.S.A.R1							1
	519	HOLSTEIN Mark G.	c/o Guaranty Trust Co. Pall Mall, London	"	LAWYER			58						U.S.A.	U.S.A.							1
	520	HOLT Carolyn R.	c/o American Express, London	"	BUYER				41					U.S.A.	U.S.A.R1							1
	521	HOTCHKISS Mollie	National City Bank of NY 11, Waterloo Place, London	"	NONE				55					U.S.A.	U.S.A.R1							1
	522	HUND Henry E.	c/o American Express London.	"	MANAGER	43								U.S.A.	U.S.A.							1
	523	HUND Emma L.	as above	"	HOUSEWIFE		40							U.S.A.	U.S.A.							1
	524	IDZUMI George	c/o Willis Faber, & Dumas 54, Leadenhall St. E.C.3.	"	INSURANCE BUSINESS			44						JAPAN	JAPAN							1
	525	KASSOVER Samuel	Victoria Hotel, London	"	MERCHANT			33						POLAND	U.S.A.R1							1
	526	KASSOVER Julius	as above	"	RADIO RETAILING			28						POLAND	U.S.A.R1							1
	527	KERR E. Coe	Guaranty Trust Co. London.	"	BROKER	44								U.S.A.	U.S.A.R1							1
	528	KERR Marian S.	as above	"	HOUSEWIFE		43							U.S.A.	U.S.A.R1							1
	529	KERR Ann	as above	"	SCHOLAR						7			U.S.A.	U.S.A.R1							1
	530	KERR Elmore C. Jr	as above	"	STUDENT			17						U.S.A.	U.S.A.R1							1
	531	KELLER Angie A.	Savoy Hotel, London	"	STUDENT				16					U.S.A.	U.S.A.R1							1
	532	KNEATH Watkin W.	c/o Royal Societies Club St. James St. London	"	BANKER			57						U.S.A.	U.S.A.							1
	533	KOCH August W.	Hotel Metropole, London	"	MERCHANT			73						U.S.A.	U.S.A.R1							1
	534	KOCH Emma A.	as above	"	NONE				69					U.S.A.	U.S.A.R1							1
	535	LAVARACK Frederick C.	Mayfair Hotel, London	"	PRESIDENT OF COMPANY			49						U.S.A.	U.S.A.							1
	536	LEE Rebecca	c/o Thos Cook & Son, London	"	NONE				38					U.S.A.	U.S.A.R1							1

33

* By Permanent Residence is to be understood residence for a year or more.
† In the case of Alien Passengers who are proceeding via the United Kingdom to a destination in some other country the country of destination should be shewn in this column.

33

Figure 10 List of alien passengers, including Oliver Hardy, on board SS *Aquitania*, travelling between New York and Southampton in July 1932 (BT 26/1001)

4.2.2 Departures, 1890–1960

Many aliens, especially those from Europe, came to the United Kingdom en-route to settling in other destinations. BT 27 contains the 'Passenger Lists, Outwards' from 1890. Earlier lists have not survived.

These give the names of all passengers leaving the UK, where the ship's eventual destination was a port outside Europe and the Mediterranean Sea. However, names of passengers who disembarked at European ports will be included in these lists. Passenger lists for ships whose voyages both began and ended within Europe are not included. For example, no lists survive for voyages between the UK and Ireland.

4.2.3 Registers of passenger lists, 1906–51

BT 32 contains names of ships for which passenger lists exist in BT 26 and BT 27. The entries are not complete, however. The earliest years have entries for a few ports only, and there are omissions. For readers hoping to find the name of a passenger in BT 26 or BT 27, they are of limited use, and may only be helpful if the name of the ship is already known. They do not contain the names of passengers, nor the destination of ships. These records are on open access in the Research Enquiries Room.

4.3 Quarantine records

Much of the work of the Privy Council Office in the eighteenth and nineteenth centuries derived from the concern of the Privy Council with quarantine. From 1720 the regulation of quarantine by order in Council was authorized by statute, and this legislation was consolidated in the Quarantine Act 1825. By 1813 the Privy Council Office included a superintendent of quarantine, and by 1840 there were quarantine establishments at the Firth of Forth, Hull, Liverpool, Milford, Portsmouth (Motherbank) and Rochester (Standgate Creek). Apart from the superintendent, quarantine work was carried out by officers of the Board of Customs though the Privy Council Office had a voice in some appointments. It was the quarantine powers of the Privy Council which led to its sponsorship of the boards of health which existed from 1805 to 1806 and from 1831 to 1832. In 1896 the Quarantine Act was repealed, and the Privy Council also lost to the Local Government Board its powers under an Act of 1876 to require the examination of persons arriving in United Kingdom ports from infected places.

Quarantine correspondence of the Privy Council Office for the period 1878 to 1896 can be found in PC 8: Original Correspondence, with indexed registers in PC 9. Further correspondence, petitions, ships' certificates of clearance, and customs reports concerning quarantine can be found in PC 1: Unbound Papers. Indexed daily registers for the period 1839 to 1860 are in miscellaneous books in PC 6/4–6. A register of reports from abroad concerning epidemics and quarantine is in PC 6/10. Entry books of out-letters, including several relating solely to quarantine, covering the period 1832–44, are in PC 7.

Customs records concerning the administration of quarantine regulations may be found in CUST 33: Extra and Intra-Departmental Correspondence, CUST 46: Registered Papers and CUST 58: Outport Records: Portsmouth. CUST 58/306–309 specifically relate to the quarantine station at Ryde, Isle of Wight.

Related Local Government Board quarantine papers can be found in MH 19: Correspondence with Government Offices and MH 20: Registers of Correspondence with Government Offices.

It is unlikely that any lists of individuals put into quarantine will be found among these records, though names of affected ports and vessels can be identified.

5 Naturalization and denization

5.1 The law of nationality

The reign of Edward III saw the first piece of English citizenship legislation. In 1335, the Act 9 Edw. III c. 1, drew a distinction between natural born English subjects and aliens. An 'alien' can be defined as a person of a foreign nation or allegiance. The Act ordered aliens residing in England to pay double the rate of taxation paid by a natural born citizen. This had the dual effect of raising extra revenue for the Crown, and of allowing the Crown some control of aliens in England.

In order to improve their position and acquire the privileges of natural born citizens, aliens resident in England could obtain either a private act of naturalization or letters of denizen.

5.1.1 Acts of naturalization

An Act of naturalization was obtained by introducing a private bill into parliament, and once enacted gave the recipient a position in all respects similar to that of a natural born citizen. All private Acts of parliament are held at the House of Lords Record Office (for address *see* Appendix 4). These records are described in Section 5.3.3.

5.1.2 Letters of denizen

The Crown could grant letters of denizen. These endowed an individual with certain privileges with effect from the date of the grant of denizen. These privileges included the ability to buy land, but not the right to inherit land. Such privileges would be passed on to children born after the grant, but not to any born before.

Letters of denizen were enrolled on Patent Rolls and are often referred to as letters patent of denization. Letters of denizen are fully described and indexed in the printed calendars of Patent Rolls which are available in the Map and Large Document Room. The terms of the letters patent of denization varied at times in accordance with the provisions of the general acts of parliament passed to govern the status of aliens residing in England. These records are described in Section 5.3.2.

5.1.3 Denization and naturalization distinctions

In a number of cases, bills passed by parliament conferring full rights to individual alien merchants were amended when the king endorsed them, to include the proviso that the grantee be required to pay a higher rate of custom levy. This ensured that the king did not lose financially by making the grant.

The terms of letters of denizen also varied in accordance with the terms of the general Acts that were passed to control the status of aliens – *see* Chapter 1. Whilst denization was granted by the king and conferred only restricted rights, Acts of naturalization were passed by parliament and offered full rights. These two distinct provisions for aliens continued to co-exist, and reflected the distinction that grants conferred by the king in person were executive Acts and grants of naturalization conveyed by the king in parliament were legislative Acts. In making his grants of denization by letters patent the king could include whatever stipulations he desired, such as whether or not a grantee would be liable to pay native or alien customs rates. However, the terms denization and naturalization were often used interchangeably in the seventeenth century and the term denization can be found in Acts of naturalization.

Nevertheless, the distinction between denization and naturalization continued until modern times. However, after 1844, the number of grants of denization decreased. They appear from the records to have been discontinued in 1873 by which time the Secretary of State of Home Affairs was authorized to grant naturalizations.

5.2   Sources for citizenship policy records

Citizenship policy documents in the PRO include general files relating to policy concerning denization, naturalization by private act of parliament, naturalization by certificate of Secretary of State, naturalization under acts of the Irish parliament, Channel Islands naturalization, colonial, and foreign naturalization.

5.2.1 Before 1940

General policy files of the Aliens Office (which administered the regulation of aliens from 1783 until 1836 when it was absorbed fully into the Home Office) have not survived.

Pre-1940 departmental policy files relating to the subject of citizenship can be found in Home Office registered papers in HO 45 and HO 144 under the subheadings 'Aliens', 'Denization', 'Nationality' and 'Naturalization'. Descriptions of these pieces can be found in the lists for these two classes which deal with a range of subjects, reflecting the diversity of matters dealt with by the Home Office. HO 162 consists of entry books of out-letters relating to various aspects (including policy matters) of the working of the Aliens Act 1905, the Aliens Restriction Act 1914 and subsequent legislation.

5.2.2 After 1940

HO 213 contains general (GEN) policy files of the Aliens Department. The files deal with the definition of British and foreign nationality, naturalizations, immigration, refugees, internees and prisoners of war, the employment of foreign labour, deportation, the status of citizens of the Irish Republic and related subjects. There are also papers relating to departmental committees, statistics, conferences, conventions and treaties on these subjects. The GEN series began in the late 1930s as 'Aliens General'. In the late 1940s it was decided to treat 'immigration (ALN)' and 'nationality (NTY)' separately and ALN and NTY file series were opened. There is an index in the contents list for this class based on Home Office registry file cuts.

In 1949 the Home Office replaced the six-figure file series of general correspondence with separate series of files for each subject or function, each distinguished by letter symbols. Legislation relating to the control of immigration and reference to nationality policy may be found in a number of classes such as:

- HO 352: Aliens, General Matters (ALG Symbol Series) Files, 1945–73;
- HO 367: Aliens Department and Immigration and Nationality Department: Organization (ALO and IMO Symbol Series) Files, 1961–2;
- HO 394: Immigration General (IMG Symbol Series) Files, 1961–75.

Some pieces within these classes include administrative histories of the departmental functions and responsibilities for immigration and citizenship policy and legislation such as: HO 352/51: The Alien Problem, memorandum by P. Conlan; HO 352/53: Aliens Control in the Nineteenth Century, memorandum by D. E. Faulkner; and HO 367/1: History of Immigration and Nationality Department (IND).

5.3 Sources for individual denization and naturalization records, 1509–1969

Very few records of individual denization and naturalization appear before 1509, the year in which King Henry VIII came to the throne, and there are no comprehensive name indexes before this date. This point is illustrated by the table below which shows the number of persons who obtained letters of denizen and acts of naturalization in each decade from 1509–1600:

Years	Number	Years	Number	Years	Number
1501–10	8	1541–50	3972	1581–90	147
1511–20	101	1551–60	487	1591–1600	75
1521–30	102	1561–70	1037		
1531–40	423	1571–80	639		

A table showing the number of persons who obtained letters of denizen or Acts of parliament in each decade in the sixteenth century. (Source: W. Page, *Letters of Denizen and Acts of Naturalisation for Aliens in England, 1509–1603*, Huguenot Society, Lymington, 1873.)

It is important to note that the vast majority of aliens settling in the United Kingdom did not go through the legal formalities of denization or naturalization as these processes were expensive and only the rich could afford them.

Throughout the period 1509 to 1969 there are three forms of record relating to denization and naturalization: firstly, memorial documents presented by the applicant wishing to gain British nationality; secondly, government departmental records concerning the application of the individual and background papers pertaining to the individual (where they survive, departmental papers are filed with the individual memorials); and finally duplicate copies of certificates of nationality presented to successful applicants and other official records such as copies of naturalization acts of parliament and denizen letters patent.

5.3.1 Documentary sources

The vast majority of documentary sources relating to the granting of British nationality can be found at the PRO. Some, however, can be found elsewhere: most notably in the House of Lords Record Office (for address *see* Appendix 4), described in Section 5.3.3.

5.3.2 Denization documentary sources

5.3.2.1 Signet Office

In the case of denization applications, an applicant would first present a petition. Such petitions do not survive for the period before 1800. What do survive from before this date are the signet bills, an impressed seal or stamp ordering the grant of denization to be drawn up. The key finding aid to these records are the Signet Office docquet books (SO 3) which contain short summaries of the signet bills kept by the clerks of the signet for the purpose of calculating the fees that were due. Contained in the docquet books are details not only of bills which gave rise to instruments sealed within the signet, but also of immediate warrants sent from the King to the Lord Chancellor, upon which the clerk levied fees, even though the warrants did not pass under the signet. The docquet books are indexed, by name of applicant, in the class SO 4.

5.3.2.2 State Paper Office and Chancery records

A duplicate series of docquet books created for the information of the Secretary of State for the period 1541–1761 can be found in SP 38, whilst the king's bills can be found in SP 39 for 1567–1645 and SO 7 for 1661–1851. The document SP 44/67 contains warrants for the denization of French Protestant refugees 1681–88.[1] The entry of grants of denization in the Patent Rolls can be found in classes C 66 and C 67 until 1844, when responsibility passed to the Home Office (a few subsequently appear). The document C 197/29 contains draft letters patent of denizations between 1830 and 1873. A small number of original letters patent of denization are found in C 97, suggesting that the documents in this class were unclaimed by the patentees. With one exception from 1830, the original patents in class C 97 all date from the period 1752–92.

5.3.2.3 Home Office

Later records relating to denization are preserved among Home Office records, notably HO 1/6–12, which contains denization papers (including petitions) and correspondence 1801–40; HO 44/44–9, which contains a sample selection of reports, petitions and affidavits for denizations, 1801–32; and HO 4, which contains original patents of denization, 1804–43. HO 5 includes out-letters and entry books of the Home Office and the Aliens Office relating to aliens and registers of applications for denization. The class covers the period 1794–1921, though between 1871 and 1873 such out-letters will be found HO 136.

5.3.3 *Naturalization documentary sources*

In the case of naturalization, the original private bills of naturalization presented to parliament from 1497 are in the custody of the House of Lords Record Office (for address *see* Appendix 4). Abstracts of these private bills of naturalization are contained in the published editions of Journals of the House of Lords and Journals of the House of Commons. Copies of these publications are held in the PRO Library and other major reference libraries. The PRO classes HO 1, HO 45 and HO 144 contain Home Office papers and memorials relating to these bills.

---

[1] These names appear in print in the Publications of the Huguenot Society of London, XVIII, and previously in the Camden Society Records [original series], LXXXII, 1862.

5.3.3.1 King's Bench and Exchequer records

Classes KB 24 and E 169/86 include lists of foreign Protestants who, under the Act of 7 Anne, c. 5, in 1708, were deemed to have become naturalized by taking the oaths of allegiance and supremacy in the open court. These records survive for the period 1708–11. Lists of those taking oaths before the Quarter Sessions may survive locally at county record offices in Quarter Session records (*see* Section 7.2.2, and Appendix 2, and also Jeremy Gibson, *Quarter Sessions Records for Family Historians*, FFHS, Birmingham, 1995).

5.3.3.2 Colonial Office and Dominions Office

Between 1740 and 1773 foreign Protestants in the Americas could also be naturalized by the taking of oaths in court and lists of those naturalized may be found in CO 5 and in the related entry books in CO 324/55–6.

Files on individuals who were granted certificates of naturalization by governments of British possessions overseas may be found in CO 323, CO 1032 and DO 35 and also relevant CO and DO country correspondence classes. Consult A. Thurston, *Sources for Colonial Studies in the Public Record Office* (London, HMSO, 1995) for further information. Duplicate certificates of naturalization for such cases may be found in HO 334. *See* Section 5.6.3.

5.3.3.3 Home Office and Court of Chancery

Later records relating to naturalization are preserved principally among Home Office records. The memorials or petitions submitted by applicants wishing to be considered for naturalization may be found in HO 1/13–176 for the period 1802–71; HO 45 for 1872–8; HO 144 for 1879–1922. Permission to view post-1922 records should be sought from the Departmental Record Officer at the Home Office (for address *see* Appendix 4).

HO 5 includes out-letters of the Home Office and the Aliens Office relating to aliens and registers of applications for naturalization. The class covers the period 1794–1921, though between 1871 and 1873 such out-letters will be found in HO 136. Further out-letters can also be found in HO 43.

Copies of certificates granted to successful applicants after the Naturalization Act 1844 may be found enrolled on the Close Rolls in C 54 for the period 1844–73 and in HO 334 between 1870 and 1969. HO 334 also includes duplicate certificates of declarations of British nationality issued under the British Nationality Act 1948 and these records survive for the period 1949–69. Permission to view post-1969 certificate records should be sought from the Departmental Record Officer at the Home Office (for address *see* Appendix 4).

Additional information regarding certificates of naturalization granted by governments of British possessions overseas such as original applications of naturalization may be found in the original correspondence classes for the colony or dominion in which the certificate was granted by referring to the relevant CO and DO class lists.

5.3.4 Name indexes to citizenship records

The central means of reference to citizenship records are the indexes to persons who successfully secured denization or naturalization during this period. These surname indexes, published or unpublished, can be found in the PRO reading rooms located alongside the HO class lists, and consist of copies of the following works: W. Page, *Denization and Naturalization of Aliens in England, 1509–1603* (Huguenot Society, vol. VIII, Lymington, 1893); W. A. Shaw, *Letters of Denizen and Acts of Naturalization for Aliens in England, 1603–1800* (Huguenot Society, Lymington, 1911, Manchester, 1923 and London, 1932); unpublished indexes compiled by Home Office departmental staff to denizations 1801–73, and to Acts of naturalization, 1801–1900; and indexes to naturalizations granted by the Secretary of State for Home Affairs, 1844–1961. Copies of yearly indexes can also be found among the series of parliamentary papers on microfiche in the Microfilm Reading Room. Although the parliamentary papers do not provide Home Office references or certificate numbers, they often list full addresses of applicants.

The information provided in these indexes varies. Huguenot Society publications provide full transcriptions of documents and those indexes listing naturalizations and denizations after 1800 do not. However, in addition to names, the denization index for 1800–73 lists country of origin and details of rights conferred and the index to naturalization by Secretary of State for 1844–1961 lists country of origin and place of residence. These indexes are a useful tool for social historians and local historians examining patterns of immigration in local communities in the nineteenth and twentieth centuries.

Although these indexes are *complete* in the sense that they claim to list *all* those persons who were successful in securing British nationality from 1509 to 1961, not all the records to which they refer survive. Remember to check variants in spelling or anglicizing of surnames. Also, if an alien changed name you may need to check under both the former name and new name. Until the beginning of 1916 aliens resident in Britain changed their names like British subjects, but enemy aliens were then forbidden by Order in Council to change their names. This rule was extended by the Aliens Restriction (Amendment) Act 1919 (as amended by reg. 20 of the Defence (General) Regulations 1939) to all aliens. Exemption was possible only when a new name was assumed by Royal Licence or by special permission of the Home Secretary, or when a woman assumed her husband's surname on marriage. Exemptions in the

Name.	Country.	Date of Certificate.	Place of Residence.	Number of Certificate.	Number of Home Office Paper.	Remarks.
Markowich, Hersel (known as Harris Markus).	Russia ...	13 June 1885 ...	Fleetwood ...	A 4314	A 39650	
Markowitch, Barnett	Russia ...	9 March 1895 ...	London	A 8260	B 17775	
Marks, Aaron ...	Prussia ...	28 December 1859 ...	... ...	3110	—	
Marks, Abraham ...	Russia ...	10 October 1894	London	A 8067	B 16633	
Marks, Abraham ...	Russia ...	7 January 1896	Manchester ...	A 8681	B 19582	
Marks, Abraham Isaac. ...	Wongrowitz	21 February 1850	... ...	1081	—	
Marks, Barnett ...	Russia ...	30 July 1894 ...	Leeds	A 7967	B 16674	
Marks, Charles ...	Russia ...	15 January 1896	London	A 8691	B 19618	
Marks, David ...	Russia ...	... ...	... ...	—	—	*See* Lindtner, David.
Marks, Edward ...	Prussia ...	5 August 1845 ...	... ...	199	—	
Marks, Edward ...	Prussia ...	11 August 1863 ...	... ...	4149	—	
Marks, Emil ...	Austria-Hungary.	... ...	... ...	—	—	*See* Mandl, Emil.
Marks, Ephraim ...	Russia ...	12 March 1896 ...	Manchester ...	A 8823	B 20407	
Marks, Gersan ...	Prussia ...	4 November 1858	... ...	2773	—	
Marks, Harris ...	Russia ...	5 January 1869	... ...	6044	—	
Marks, Harris ...	Russian-Poland.	1 June 1886 ...	London	A 4593	A 43267	
Marks, Harris ...	Russia ...	19 January 1887	London	A 5212	A 45773	
Marks, Harris ...	Russia ...	29 August 1894 ...	Leeds	A 8026	B 16654	
Marks, Harry Hananel.	United States of America.	28 April 1888 ...	London	D 36	B 3011	
Marks, Henry ...	Prussia ...	2 August 1889 ...	... ...	—	—	*See* Marcus, Herman.
Marks, Hermann ...	Germany ...	28 June 1875 ...	... ...	A 1641	45506	
Marks, James ...	Poland ...	2 April 1850 ...	... ...	1095	—	
Marks, John ...	Russian Poland.	1 November 1859	... ...	3069	—	
Marks, Joseph ...	Prussia ...	9 July 1852 ...	... ...	1394	—	
Marks, Joseph ...	Russia ...	15 February 1897	London	A 9482	B 22843	
Marks, Julius ...	Russia ...	10 September 1886	London	A 4878	A 44551	
Marks, Julius ...	Russia ...	15 September 1897	London	A 9840	B 24482	
Marks, Kaufman ...	Prussia ...	4 November 1858	... ...	2774	—	
Marks, Leon ...	Prussia ...	29 December 1853	... ...	1709	—	
Marks, Levi ...	Poland ...	20 July 1848 ...	... ...	852	—	
Marks, Michael ...	Russia ...	5 May 1897 ...	Manchester ...	A 9621	B 23729	

CERTIFICATES OF NATURALIZATION. 215

Figure 11 Index to naturalizations, 1800–1900, with entry for Michael Marks (of Marks and Spencer fame), 1897

first two classes were advertised in the *London Gazette*. There are now no restrictions attached to a change of name effected in the United Kingdom by an overseas national. The parts of the Aliens Restriction (Amendment) Act relating to this were repealed by the Statute Law (Repeal) Act 1971. The Defence (General) Regulations lapsed some years previously.

HO 5 includes out-letters and entry books of the Home Office and the Aliens Office relating to aliens and registers of applications for denization. The class covers the period 1794 to 1921, though between 1871 and 1873, such out-letters will be found in HO 136. These records include registers of applications for naturalization for the period 1798–1829 (HO 5/34–7), which record name of applicant, date of arrival in the United Kingdom, place of residence and date of certificate if granted.

Name indexes to naturalization do not include unsuccessful applicants. For memorial records relating to persons falling into this category *see* Section 5.4.7.

5.4 Tracing memorial records

5.4.1 *Memorial records: general characteristics*

Memorial documents and background departmental records are filed together to form one record. Memorial records consist of a petition by the applicant and, in many instances, an affidavit supporting the application. Departmental records may include investigations carried out by local authorities concerning the suitability of the candidate. Before any general naturalization legislation was introduced in 1844, and before the Home Office became actively involved in the granting of naturalizations, there were no general requirements to govern the content of the memorial. Following the 1844 Act, every alien who had the intention of becoming a British citizen was required to present a memorial to the Secretary of State stating age, trade and duration of residence. Following an Act of 1 August 1847, regulations provided that a declaration should be made and signed by at least four householders, who should state their places of residence, vouch for the respectability and loyalty of the applicant, and verify the several particulars stated in the memorial. The householders, known as resident referees, were required to make their declarations before a magistrate. Resident referees were accepted only if they met the following criteria: they were natural born British subjects; were not the agents or solicitors of the applicant; were able to testify to the facts of residence from personal knowledge; and had known the applicant for at least five years.

The 1870 Act required further information. It introduced a qualification period, demanding that applicants should reside within the United Kingdom for at least five years before submitting an application, in addition to declaring their intention to reside permanently in the country. After 1870, memorialist records include name and address of memorialist, names and addresses of any children residing with him or her and the addresses of any residences occupied by him or her during the five year qualification period. From 1880 an additional resident referee was required specifically to verify the times and addresses and periods of residence required for the five year qualification period.

After 1873, following communication between the Metropolitan Police Commissioner and the Secretary of State about certain Belgians and Germans who had committed offences in their respective countries and attempted to apply for naturalization so as to avoid extradition from the United Kingdom, the practice of obtaining a Metropolitan Police report on the respectability of the applicant and the referees was established. Outside London, mayors, and chairmen of Quarter Sessions were asked to inquire into the respectability of candidates and their referees.

The 1914 Act introduced the requirement for candidates to have an adequate knowledge of English, and memorials after this Act include English proficiency tests.

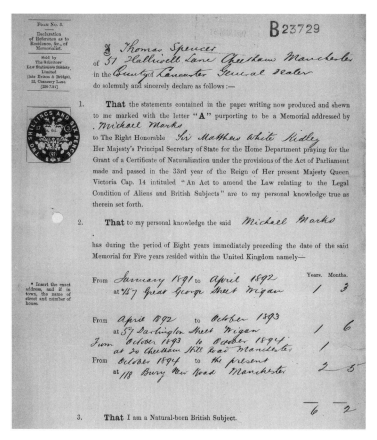

Figure 12 Naturalization papers for Michael Marks (of Marks and Spencer fame), 1897, includes Thomas Spencer as a resident referee (HO 144/407/B23729)

5.4.2 1509–1800

No memorial papers survive for this period. The only records of individual naturalizations and denizations for this period are the individual private Acts of naturalization and denizen letters patent – *see* Section 5.5 for details.

5.4.3 Denizations, 1801–73

For denizations, check the alphabetical name index to lists of denizens by letters patent, 1801–73. There are three sources of Home Office background papers and memorial papers for this period:

- HO 1/6–12 for patents issued 1801–40
- HO 44/44–9 for patents issued 1801–32 (within the HO 44 class list there is a separate index to persons, corporate bodies and places which provides folio references within documents)

- HO 45 for patents issued 1841–73. (The piece number for this class is simply converted from the 'OS' – Old Series – number listed in the 'HO number' column.)

5.4.4 Naturalization by Act of parliament, 1802–1900

Begin your search by checking the alphabetical name index for naturalizations by Act of parliament between 1802 and 1900 among the HO class lists. There are three sources of memorial papers for this period:

- HO 1/13–16 for correspondence 1802–58
- HO 45 for correspondence 1841–78. (The piece numbers for memorials in this class is simply the cited 'OS' – Old Series – number between 1841 and 1871 and, after 1872 is derived from the HO 45 Packing List – *see* Appendix 1.)
- HO 144 for correspondence 1879–1900. (The piece numbers for memorials in this class are derived from the HO 144 Packing List – *see* Appendix 1.)

Please note that the index represents years as *regnal* years, e.g. 42 Geo. 3, which is 25 October 1801 to 24 October 1802. To convert regnal years to calendar years consult C.

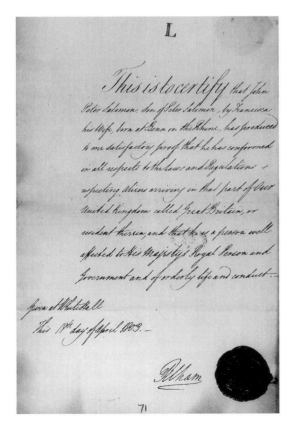

Figure 13 Denization certificate of Peter Salomon, 1803 (HO 44/45)

R. Cheney's *Handbook of Dates*, (Cambridge University Press, 1996) available in the Research Enquiries Room.

5.4.5 Naturalization granted by the Home Office, 1844–1922

Begin your search by checking the alphabetical name index for naturalizations granted by the Secretary of State for Home Affairs 1844–1935 among the HO class lists. There are three sources for memorial papers for this period:

- HO 1/17–176 for correspondence 1844–71. (The full piece reference for memorials in this class are derived by matching up the Certificate number quoted in the index with the HO 1 class list.)
- HO 45 for correspondence 1872–8. (The full piece references for memorials in this class are derived by matching up the HO Paper number quoted in the index with the HO 45 Packing List – *see* Appendix 1.)
- HO 144 for correspondence 1879–1924. (The full piece references for memorials in this class are derived by matching up the HO Paper number quoted in the index with the HO 144 Packing List – *see* Appendix 1.)

Occasionally, post-1879 files may be found in HO 45 and pre-1879 ones in HO 144 so it is best to check both sources. Also, if an individual case was re-opened by the Home Office at any time after the year of naturalization, the case would then be filed away at a new, later, date. Additional finding aids to Home Office twentieth century naturalization indexes can help explain seemingly missing files. These are located in the Research Enquiries Room. Home Office correspondence rarely survives for naturalizations granted by Governors of British possessions overseas though memorial papers for selected cases can be found in CO 323 and DO 35 particularly for the period 1930–1950. Few cases appear to be cleared for public inspection.

5.4.6 Tracing memorial records after 1922

Memorial papers for naturalizations after 1922 are closed to public inspection but those for persons naturalized between 1923 and 1934 may be opened on application for review to the Departmental Record Officer of the Home Office (for address *see* Appendix 4.) Applications are accepted in writing only. Remember to quote the full HO 144 document reference when applying. The Home Office is opening an increasing number of records before 1934 but some records will remain closed to maintain confidentiality. Since the basis for closure is usually the personal sensitivity of the information – and this is generally only regarded as sensitive for the lifetime of the individual – researchers who can provide evidence that the individual is dead will be assisting the Home Office considerably in determining whether the file can be opened, although there may, of course, be continuing sensitivities in regard to other people mentioned in the file.

HO 405 will be the class of records for all the post-1934 applications for naturalization made by people who arrived in the UK before 1948 where the file has survived. This represents an estimated 40 per cent of all such cases so the collection constitutes a very large sample, preserved exceptionally to show the handling of refugees in a period of political turmoil. These records are due for transfer to the PRO over the next few years. On transfer these files will be closed but, as with all their records at the PRO, the Home Office will review the closure of individual files on request. These 1934–48 files are being transferred under a ten year programme in alphabetical order, so all those with surnames beginning with 'A' will be transferred before those beginning with 'B' regardless of date. The first transfer of records is due in 2000. All files will be closed for 100 years, though the Home Office will review files on request subject to resources. Until all the files have been transferred and opened, the Home Office will continue to respond to enquiries from researchers as at present. In addition they have begun sensitivity reviews of some of the more famous of the representative cases with a view to opening them in full or in part, possibly during 2000.

It will be many years before all the files are at the PRO and many more before they are fully available.

There are *very* occasionally old papers attached and the date range can be wide (especially as applications have been preserved *as well as* acceptances). The files will be closed for 100 years on transfer but files may be opened on application for review to the Home Office. The same considerations apply to the opening of these files as to those held in HO 144.

5.4.7 Tracing unsuccessful applications

The vast majority of files relating to unsuccessful applications for naturalization have not been preserved as archives. Where they survive they can be found, together with departmental papers, in HO 45 for between 1844 and 1879 and HO 144 for after 1879. There is no complete index to these records and references to any surviving records may be found in the list relating to the subject heading 'Naturalization', in the main lists for both these classes rather than in the separate indexes to naturalizations.

HO 5 includes out-letters and entry books of the Home Office and the Aliens Office relating to aliens and registers of applications for denization. The class covers the period 1794 to 1921, though for between 1871 and 1873, such out-letters will be found in HO 136. These records include registers of applications for naturalization for the period 1798–1829 (HO 5/34–7), which record name of applicant, date of arrival in the

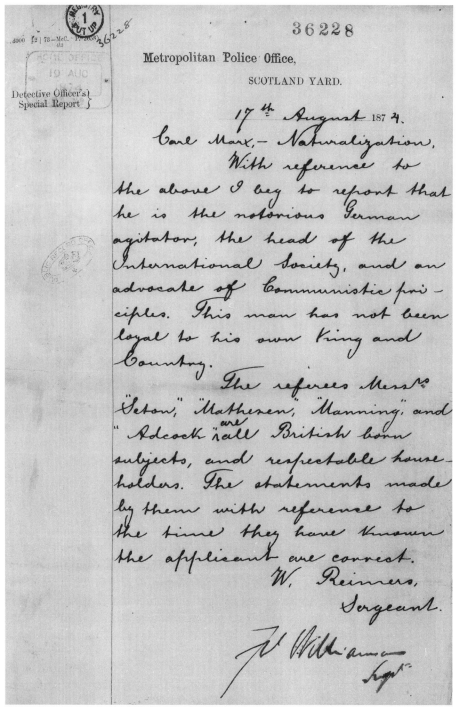

Figure 14 Police report recommending the refusal to grant naturalization to Carl Marx, 1874 (HO 45/9366/36228)

United Kingdom, place of residence and date of certificate if granted. The class also includes correspondence relating to unsuccessful applicants. Not all pieces include a nominal index.

As mentioned in Section 5.4.6, unsuccessful applications are included in the files due to be transferred to HO 405. Many successful applicants made previous unsuccessful applications and in these cases all the applications survive. Those applications made between 1934 and 1948 are being transferred under a ten year programme in alphabetical order, so all those with surnames beginning with 'A' will be transferred before those with 'B' regardless of date. The first transfer of records is due in 2000. All files will be closed for 100 years, though the Home Office will review files on request subject to resources (*see* Section 5.4.6).

5.5 Tracing Acts of parliament and letters patent

5.5.1 General characteristics

These documents are official government records recording the fact that citizenship rights were granted to individuals. Later records are often required as legal evidence to prove that naturalization was granted and where any other official copy had been lost. Individuals often need to present proof that citizenship rights were conferred in order to obtain other documents and entitlements such as passports, marriage certificates and to prove pensions rights. Information provided in these documents is usually restricted to full name, country of origin and the date when citizenship rights were conferred and – for the period before 1800 – such information has been included in the index to names (*see* Section 5.3.2.)

5.5.2 Denizations by letters patent, 1509–1873

For denizations by letters patent before 1800, consult W. Page, *Denization and Naturalization of Aliens in England, 1509–1603* (Huguenot Society, vol. VIII, Lymington, 1893) and W. A. Shaw, *Letters of Denizen and Acts of Naturalization for Aliens in England, 1603–1800* (Huguenot Society, Lymington, 1911, Manchester, 1923 and London, 1932). These publications can be found among the Home Office (HO) class lists in the reading rooms on the open shelves and the publications include full transcriptions of the denization records themselves. The indexes contain transcriptions of those records detailed in Section 5.3.2 and cite full PRO document references.

In order to trace an entry for letters patent for denizations after 1800 you will need to refer to a series of finding aids to Patent Rolls and other Chancery Rolls known as Palmer's Indexes in IND 1/17276–428. The indexes are arranged chronologically. The indexes refer to entries of denization by letters patent entered on the Patent Rolls and supplementary Patent Rolls in C 66 and C 67 between 1801 and 1844, when responsibility passed to the Home Office (a few subsequently appear). Draft letters patent for denizations between 1830 and 1873 can be found in C 197/29.

A roll of warrants for letters of denizen for the city of Westminster is held at the Westminster Abbey Muniments and Library (*see* Appendix 4 for address).

5.5.3 Naturalizations by Act of parliament, 1509–1900

Before 1800, consult W. Page, *Denization and Naturalization of Aliens in England, 1509–1603* (Huguenot Society, vol. VIII, Lymington, 1893) and W. A. Shaw, *Letters of Denizen and Acts of Naturalization for Aliens in England, 1603–1800* (Huguenot Society, Lymington, 1911, Manchester, 1923 and London, 1932). These publications can be found among the Home Office (HO) class lists in the reading rooms on the open shelves and the publications include transcriptions of the naturalization records themselves including naturalizations by private Act of parliament, the original records being housed at the House of Lords Record Office (*see* Appendix 4 for address).

For Acts after 1900, consult *Index to Local and Personal Acts* (London, HMSO, 1949), a copy of which is held in the PRO Library. Once again, copies of the Acts may be found in the House of Lords Record Office. Abstracts of these private Acts of naturalization are contained in the published editions of Journals of the House of Lords and Journals of the House of Commons. Copies of these publications are held in the PRO Library.

5.6 Tracing citizenship certificate records 1844–1969

5.6.1 Certificate records: general characteristics

Certificate documents consist of departmental copies of the certificates of naturalization or British nationality issued to successful applicants. Essentially, the certificate document contains a summary of information supplied in the memorial itself, namely: name of applicant, address, trade or occupation, place and date of birth, nationality, marital status, name of spouse (if applicable) and names and nationalities of parents. Between 1844 and 1873 certificates of naturalization were copied onto parchment and the copies then enrolled on the Close Rolls. After 1870 they were bound together in volumes (usually of 500 certificates) in the Home Office. Duplicate copies of certificates of British nationality after the British Nationality Act 1948 are also filed in this way.

5.6.2 Naturalization certificates 1844–70

Certificates of naturalization granted by the Secretary of State were enrolled on the Court of Chancery Close Rolls (C 54) from August 1844 to August 1873. In order to trace entries for certificates of naturalization for these dates you will first need to find the date of certificate provided in the index to naturalizations and then refer to a series of finding aids to Close Rolls and other Chancery Rolls, known as Palmer's Indexes, in IND 1/17276–428. The indexes are arranged chronologically.

5.6.3 Naturalization certificates 1870–1969

Begin your search by consulting the name indexes to naturalizations, which can be found among the HO class lists up to and including the year 1936, among the series of Additional Finding Aids in the Research Enquiries Room for the period 1937–57, and among the series of parliamentary papers on microfiche in the Microfilm Reading Room for certificates issued between 1958 and 1961. Please note, indexes for certificates issued after 1961 are held by the Home Office – *see* Appendix 4 for address.

There is only one record class of certificates referred to in these indexes and that is HO 334, which contains duplicates of certificates and declarations granted by the Home Secretary under the Naturalization Act 1870, the British Nationality and Status of Aliens Act 1914, and British Nationality Act 1948. The various types of certificates granted under these Acts are explained in Appendix 3.

Having identified a name in the index to naturalizations, match up the certificate number with the corresponding piece reference in the HO 334 list – certificates in this class are filed together, usually in volumes of 500 certificates. It is therefore important to remember the certificate number so you can find the right certificate when the document arrives.

5.6.4 Registration of British citizenship documents 1948–69

These documents are generally known as 'R' certificates and refer to registrations of British citizenship declared by a British subject or citizen of the Republic of Ireland or of the Channel Islands, Isle of Man, a colony, a protectorate or a protected state, or a UK Trust Territory. The distinctions between the various 'R' categories are listed in Appendix 3.

'R' certificates were issued under the British Nationality Act 1948 and duplicate Home Office copies may be found in the class HO 334. *See* Section 2.5 for further information.

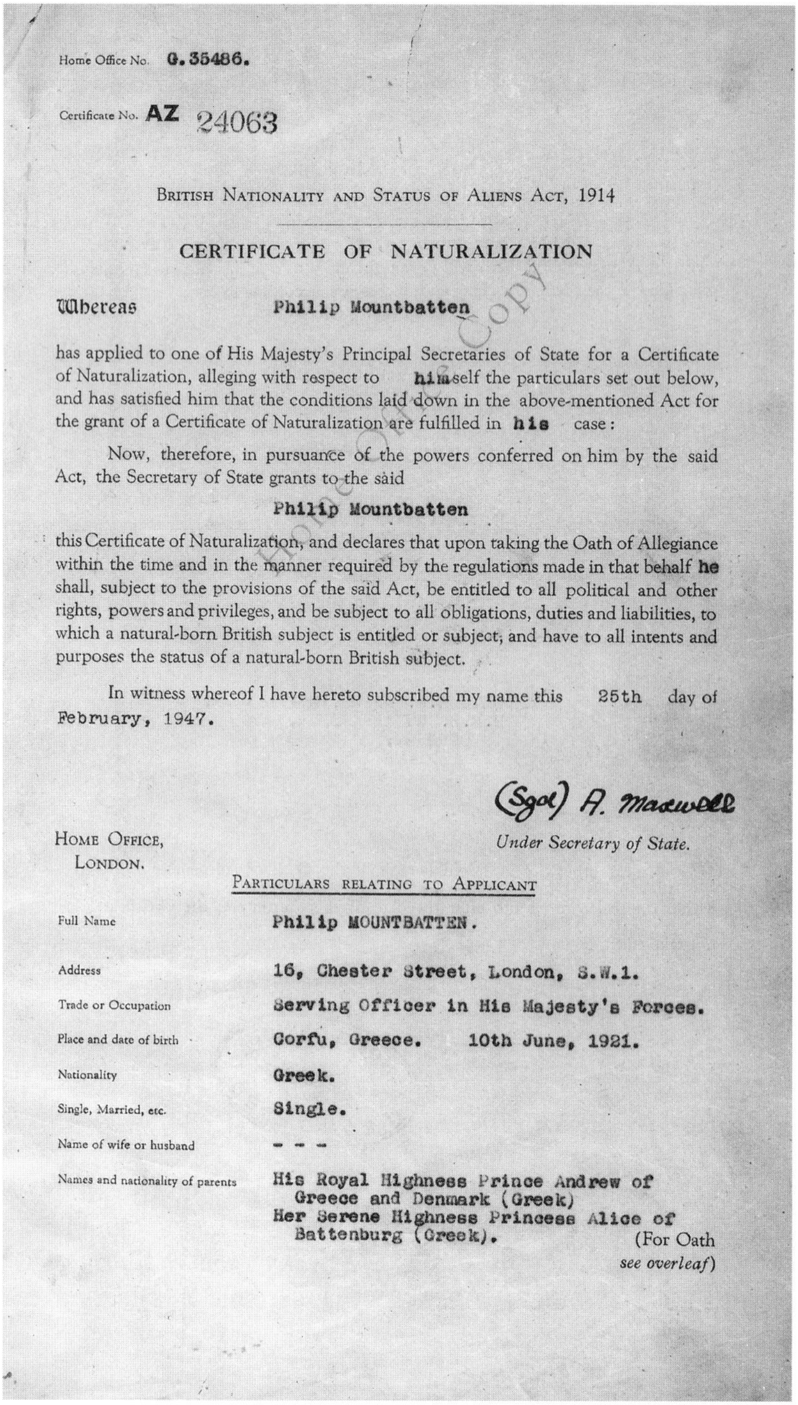

Home Office No. **G.35486.**

Certificate No. **AZ** 24063

BRITISH NATIONALITY AND STATUS OF ALIENS ACT, 1914

CERTIFICATE OF NATURALIZATION

Whereas   **Philip Mountbatten**

has applied to one of His Majesty's Principal Secretaries of State for a Certificate of Naturalization, alleging with respect to   **him**self the particulars set out below, and has satisfied him that the conditions laid down in the above-mentioned Act for the grant of a Certificate of Naturalization are fulfilled in **his**   case:

Now, therefore, in pursuance of the powers conferred on him by the said Act, the Secretary of State grants to the said

Philip Mountbatten

this Certificate of Naturalization, and declares that upon taking the Oath of Allegiance within the time and in the manner required by the regulations made in that behalf **he** shall, subject to the provisions of the said Act, be entitled to all political and other rights, powers and privileges, and be subject to all obligations, duties and liabilities, to which a natural-born British subject is entitled or subject; and have to all intents and purposes the status of a natural-born British subject.

In witness whereof I have hereto subscribed my name this   25th   day of February, 1947.

(Sgd) A. Maxwell

Under Secretary of State.

HOME OFFICE,
   LONDON.

PARTICULARS RELATING TO APPLICANT

Full Name   **Philip MOUNTBATTEN.**

Address   **16, Chester Street, London, S.W.1.**

Trade or Occupation   **Serving Officer in His Majesty's Forces.**

Place and date of birth   **Corfu, Greece.   10th June, 1921.**

Nationality   **Greek.**

Single, Married, etc.   **Single.**

Name of wife or husband   **- - -**

Names and nationality of parents   **His Royal Highness Prince Andrew of
      Greece and Denmark (Greek)
    Her Serene Highness Princess Alice of
      Battenburg (Greek).**   (For Oath
                          see overleaf)

Figure 15 Home Office naturalization certificate of Philip Mountbatten, 1947 (HO 334/174 (AZ 24063))

5.6.5 *Tracing records after 1969*

All certificate records made after 1969 are in the custody of the Home Office (for address *see* Appendix 4).

5.7 Other citizenship records

Many aliens needed to submit declarations of alienage to the Home Office. Before a declaration could be registered, a certificate from some official authority, such as a consul, needed to be obtained to prove that the declaration was genuine. Surviving declarations of alienage registrations and correspondence can be found in HO 45 under the sub-heading 'Nationality and Naturalization'. Some, subject to extended closure, may also be found in HO 144 – *see* Appendix 1 for an explanation of how to use this class.

Also included in these classes is correspondence relating to certificates of British origin and special certificates of British origin, issued to coloured seamen, following the Special Restriction (Coloured Alien Seamen) Order, 1925.

6 Tracing immigrant communities

There are a number of classes of records that can be consulted to trace different immigrant communities. The sources listed below such as Home Office papers, census returns, Poor Law correspondence, soldiers' documents and seamen's records can be used to find people of different national and ethnic groups and not just those communities covered in this chapter.

6.1 Irish migration and settlement

Irish migration from the middle ages was in the form of seasonal visits for economic reasons to England. These were eventually replaced by permanent settlement from the eighteenth century, and the great movement of people in the nineteenth century.

6.1.1 Privy Council and Home Office papers

Privy Council (PC) records contain papers relating to many different subjects. The most useful class PC 1: Miscellaneous Unbound Papers includes reports on the Irish in England and the meetings of the United Irishmen in London.

Home Office (HO) papers contain many documents relating to the Irish in Britain. Many of the matters relate to political gatherings and the meetings of Irish clubs in London and other parts of the country. Correspondence on disturbances, riots and political activities can be found in HO 40: Disturbances Correspondence 1812–1855, and HO 41: Disturbances Entry Books. Most of the records in HO 41 contain a subject index. HO 45: Registered Correspondence and HO 144: Registered Correspondence, Supplementary contain general correspondence on a variety of domestic issues. These classes may be searched by subject heading, the relevant headings being Ireland and Ireland (Fenians). HO 52: Counties Correspondence contains reports of local conditions, including riots, arson and other civil disturbances. Registrations of British citizenship declared by a British subject or citizen of the Republic of Ireland between 1948 and 1969 can be found in HO 334. *See* Section 2.5 for further information.

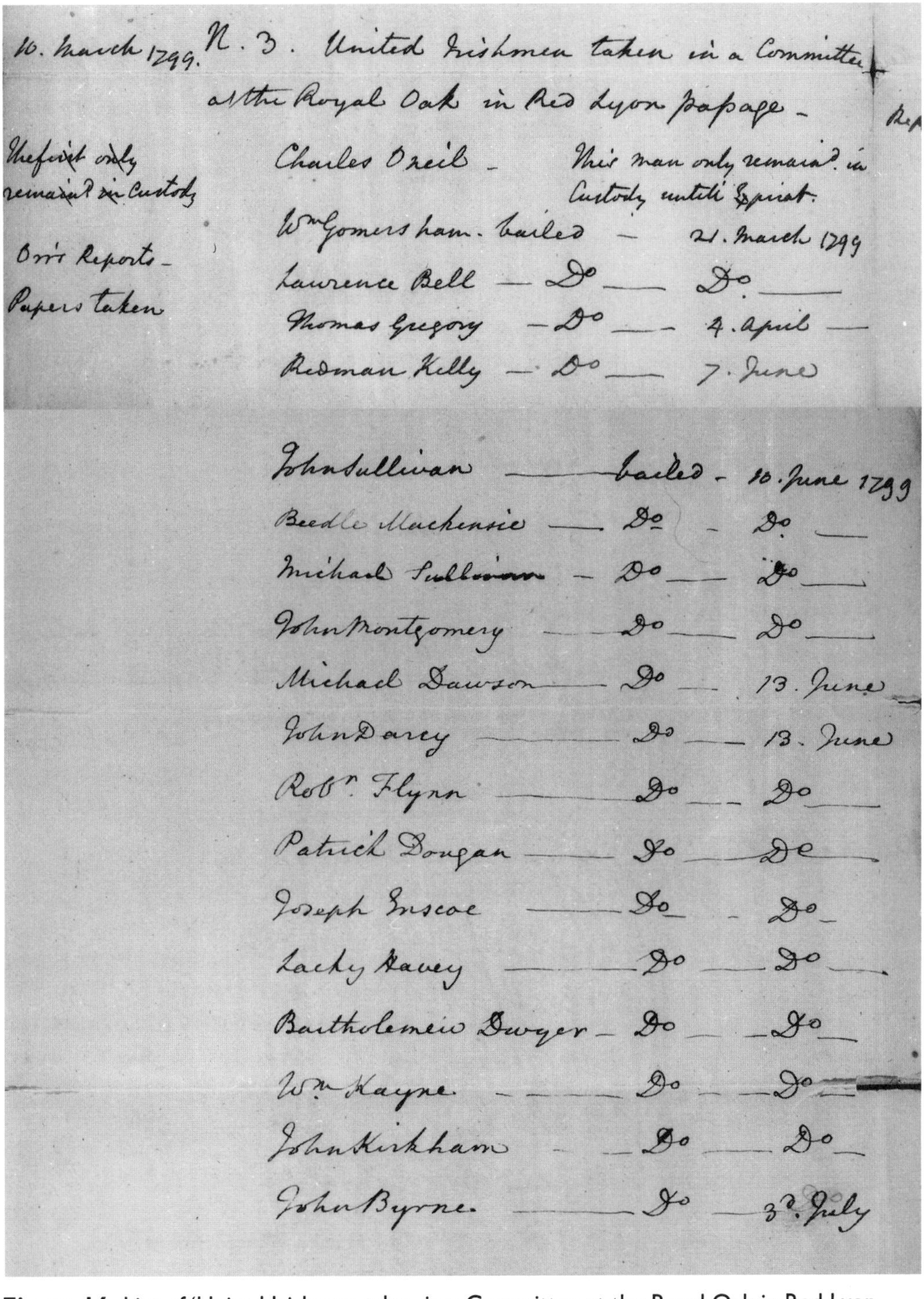

10. March 1799. N. 3. United Irishmen taken in a Committee at the Royal Oak in Red Lyon passage -

The first only remain'd in Custody

Orr's Reports -
Papers taken

Charles O'Neil	This man only remain'd in Custody untill Expiat.	
Wm Gomersham	bailed	21. March 1799
Laurence Bell	Do	Do
Thomas Gregory	Do	4. April
Redman Kelly	Do	7. June
John Sullivan	bailed	10. June 1799
Beedle Mackensie	Do	Do
Michael Sullivan	Do	Do
John Montgomery	Do	Do
Michael Dawson	Do	13. June
John Darcy	Do	13. June
Robt. Flynn	Do	Do
Patrick Dougan	Do	Do
Joseph Inscoe	Do	Do
Lacky Havey	Do	Do
Bartholemew Dwyer	Do	Do
Wm Kayne	Do	Do
John Kirkham	Do	Do
John Byrne	Do	3d. July

Figure 16 List of 'United Irishmen taken in a Committee at the Royal Oak in Red Lyon Passage', 10 March 1799 (PC 1/44/158)

6.1.2 *Census returns*

Census records for England and Wales can be consulted at the Family Records Centre. RG 11: 1881 Census Returns is the best class to start searching because it has a comprehensive index available at the Family Records Centre. You can search by county, surname and also by birthplace. In many cases place of birth will be given as Ireland, but sometimes the county is also recorded. If a family can be found in the 1881 census then other censuses should be searched for the same area: HO 107: 1841 and 1851 Census Returns and RG 9–12: 1861 to 1891 Census Returns. The 1901 census returns will be made available online in January 2002. If you cannot find a family located in the same area, other areas with known Irish communities should be searched. These communities had close ties and tended to stick together. Newly arrived immigrants would follow in the footsteps of former neighbours and friends from Ireland and often settle in the same area.

6.1.3 *Poor Law records*

MH 12: Correspondence with Poor Law Unions and other Local Authorities, contains papers concerning the whole field of Poor Law and (after 1871) local government and public health administration. These records are arranged alphabetically by county and union, so to find papers relating to a particular municipal borough or other local authority it is necessary to know in which Poor Law union it was situated (see below). Registers to this correspondence have not survived, but indexes of selected subjects dealt with in the correspondence can be found in MH 15: Subject Indexes of Correspondence. The Gibson Guides (see below) list what correspondence survives in MH 12 for each union.

A town or parish can be looked for in the 1851 census index under the county and the registration district is given. The Poor Law unions were used as the basis of civil registration districts in 1837, so the registration district given on a birth, marriage or death certificate or in the indexes at the Family Records Centre will show you in which union an event took place. Records of the unions themselves, the boards of guardians and individual workhouses, where they survive, will be held locally, see J. Gibson, *Poor Law Union Records* (4 vols, Gibson Guides, 1993) and Appendix 2.

6.1.4 *Soldiers' documents*

WO 97: Royal Hospital Chelsea: Soldiers Service Documents for non-commissioned officers and other ranks discharged up to 1913 contains the service records, attestation papers, medical records, and discharge documents of many men who served in the British Army. Though many Irish soldiers were recruited in Ireland and after service returned there, others were recruited in England and settled here after they were discharged. For soldiers who discharged between 1760 and 1854, there is a database searchable by name in the Microfilm Reading Room. For those who discharged between 1855 and 1872, the records are arranged alphabetically by name within regiment or corps. In order to trace a soldier's record for this period, it is necessary to know in which regiment or corps he served. From 1873 to 1882 the records are alphabetical by cavalry, artillery, infantry and corps, and from 1883 to 1913 alphabetical by surname for the whole army. First World War and soldiers' service records may be found in WO 363 and WO 364. Both classes are available on microfilm in the Microfilm Reading Room. For further information on army records consult *Army Records for Family Historians* (PRO Readers' Guide No. 2, 1998).

6.1.5 Canal and railway companies

Another source is canal and railway company records, particularly those records relating to the construction of lines on which many Irish labourers were employed as navvies. The Railway Department of the Board of Trade was established in 1840; it assumed responsibility for canals in the 1850s. Board of Trade papers relating to canals can be found in BT 22: Railway Department Correspondence and Papers, BT 13: Establishment Department Correspondence and Papers, BT 15: Finance Department Registered Files and BT 58: Companies Department Correspondence and Papers. The Board of Trade Railway Department records were inherited by the Ministry of Transport in 1919 and its correspondence and papers can be found in MT 6 and MT 11, and minute books in MT 13.

Records of canal and railway companies are to be found in the records formerly held at the British Transport Historical Records section (BTHR) which now form the RAIL, AN, and some ZLIB, and ZPER groups of records. Record classes relating to particular canal companies are arranged alphabetically by company name and form the classes RAIL 800–99, RAIL 1112, RAIL 1116–17, RAIL 1162–3 and RAIL 1168–71. Record classes relating to individual railway companies are arranged alphabetically by company name and form the classes RAIL 1–799 and RAIL 1175–88. Books and pamphlets on canals, railways and associated subjects are in the ZLIB classes and periodicals in the ZPER classes. A 'How to Use' leaflet concerning these records is available at the Research Enquiries Desk.

6.2 The Jewish community

Following the expulsion of the Jews from Spain in 1492 a number of Marranos or New Christians (Jews who had nominally accepted the Christian faith) came northwards to France, The Netherlands, Germany and England. A small group of Portuguese Jews settled in London in the reign of Queen Elizabeth I. Because of their commercial connections and hatred of Spain, a number of these Marranos were useful to the English government and the Elizabethan intelligence service. PC 2: Privy Council Registers and SP 12: State Papers Domestic Elizabeth I should be consulted using *Acts of the Privy Council* and the *Calendar of State Papers, Domestic; Elizabeth*. Copies of these can be found in the Map and Large Document Room.

6.2.1 Resettlement

In 1656 the Lord Protector, Oliver Cromwell, permitted Jews to resettle in England. The Council of State granted passes of safe conduct to Manasseh ben Israel, scholar and rabbi of Amsterdam. He arrived in October 1655 and presented himself to the Council, but it was not until 13 November that his petition was heard and the Council resolved 'that the Jews deserving it may be admitted into this nation to trade and traffic and dwell amongst us as Providence shall give occasion' (SP 18/101 f.115). The petition and a humble address were referred to a committee of the Council for consideration.

The petition asked that the Jews might be permitted to live in England, have synagogues and cemeteries, and trade freely. Jewish disputes were to be settled by Mosaic law and all laws against the Jews would be repealed. It was quickly decided by the lawyers that there was no legal bar to re-admission. The committee made its report to the Council of State (SP 18/101 f.118) setting out the objections made at the conference, but also reporting that there was no legal bar to the admission, though they laid down several conditions.

The legal position of the Marranos was brought to a head by the arrest of one of them, Antonio Robles, who was arrested as an enemy alien on the outbreak of war with Spain. The case brought the Marranos resident in London out into the open. After a thorough investigation, the Council of State discharged Robles and ordered the return of his goods. While his case was being heard, Manasseh ben Israel and six leading Marranos residents in London threw off their disguise and petitioned the Lord Protector as Jews asking for permission in writing for Jews to meet for worship in their houses and to bury their dead outside the city (SP 18/125 f.58). No reply or order of the Council of State appears to be extant, but the Jews must have received some assurance as they continued to live in London. In December 1656 they rented land in Creechurch Lane for a synagogue and later bought land for a cemetery.

6.2.2 Jewish immigration

The immigrants arriving from the 1650s were Sephardi (Portuguese, Spanish and Italian) and later during the 1680s Ashkenazi (central and eastern European) who arrived in the 1680s from Holland and Bohemia (the main influx of Ashkenazim from Russia and Poland was not until the end of the nineteenth century). By about 1690 there were enough German Jews for a separate Ashkenazi community in the city of London. Their first synagogue, the Great Synagogue, was opened in 1722.

SP 37: State Papers, Domestic, George III contain material on Jewish immigration in the 1770s. HO 45: Home Office: Registered Files includes material on the immigration of German, Polish and Russian Jews, 1887–1905. MEPO 2: Correspondence and Papers of the Commissioner of the Metropolitan Police contains material on landing of Jewish immigrants, work of Jewish charities and settlement of immigrant Jews in the East End of London, 1887–1905. Aliens certificates under the Aliens Act 1793 were destroyed before 1836, but those under the 1836 act survive in the following classes: HO 2: Home Office Aliens Act 1836: Certificates of Aliens for 1836–52 and HO 3: Home Office Aliens Act 1836: Returns and Papers for 1836–69 (*see* Section 4.1.3). Aliens correspondence generally will be found in HO 1 or in Domestic Correspondence (HO 42, HO 44, HO 45); out-letters on aliens matter generally in Aliens Entry Books (HO 5) 1794–1921 and on the working of the Aliens Act 1905 in Aliens Restriction: Entry Books (HO 162) 1905–21. For denization and naturalization of Jewish settlers *see* Chapter 5, and for changes of names *see* Domestic Records Information leaflet 77. Jewish settlement in the nineteenth century can be studied from the decennial census returns of 1841 to 1891 (HO 107 and RG 9-RG 12), providing demographic and residential data for the Jewish community as well as identifying individual families. These records are available at the Family Records Centre. As with the Irish, the Poor Law Board and Local Government Board correspondence (MH 12) with local Poor Law authorities in areas of Jewish settlement may be worth consulting.

6.2.3 Other sources

Genealogical records of the Jewish community from the period of resettlement onwards are not held in the Public Record Office. The London Metropolitan Archives (LMA) hold records of a number of organizations of local, national and international significance, but very few genealogical records. The Bevis Marks Hall has a collection of Jewish registers from 1687 to 1837 (*see* Appendix 4 for addresses of these archives). The records of the Board of Deputies of British Jews, the representative body of British Jewry, are held in the LMA (ref. ACC/3121) but are only available with the permission of the Board of Deputies. The Board was founded in 1760 as the London Committee of Deputies of British Jews, when representatives of the Sephardi and Ashkenazi communities in London met to present a loyal address to George III on his accession to the throne.

For other records in the Public Record Office, the State Papers up to 1782 should be consulted (*see* Domestic Records Information leaflets 15–20), followed by Home Office papers, in Domestic Correspondence, George III–Victoria (HO 42, HO 43); out-letters, 1782–1921 (HO 43, HO 136, HO 152); and the Registered Files (HO 45) from 1839 and Registered Files, Supplementary (HO 144) which are normally closed for 100 years. Probate records of the Prerogative Court of Canterbury (PROB) contain wills, administrations and related documents of prominent Jewish families and extracts have been published by the Jewish Genealogical Society of Great Britain (*see* Appendix 4 for address). Additional information about the estates of leading Jews for the eighteenth and nineteenth centuries may be found in IR 26: Estate Duty Office: Registers of Legacy Duty, Succession Duty and Estate Duty. These records cover local as well as central probates.

Jewish records are also held elsewhere. Most of the refugees settled in or around London and the records of the Jewish Temporary Shelter are available at the LMA. Other personal files of approximately 400,000 Jewish refugees are still kept by the Jewish Refugees Committee. Further information on Jewish immigrants is available at the Hartley Library at the University of Southampton, and at the Manchester Local Studies Unit. *See* Appendix 4 for addresses of these archives. Access to these archives may be restricted. Also, the Chief Rabbi's Office hold case files of adoptions, conversions, divorces and also certificates of evidence for much of the nineteenth and twentieth centuries. With the exception of the certificates of evidence, all series of documents are confidential and information will only be sent to those with a legitimate legal interest. The certificates of evidence were required by the Chief Rabbi to authorize marriages and they contain details of the applicant's date, age and place of birth and/or marriage abroad. The certificates often contain additional information to these issued by the Registrar General's Office and are particularly useful for tracing Jews who did not naturalize, where information about their origin or marriage abroad may not exist elsewhere. The Office only accepts visits by prior appointment. *See* appendix 4 for address.

For later twentieth century records concerning Jewish immigration, *see* Section 3.4.2. For medieval Jewish records, *see* Section 8.2.

6.3 The black community

The first black settlement in Britain began in the sixteenth century as a result of voyages to Africa and the development of the slave trade. Africans became increasingly common in the ports of England. One of the earliest references, however, is not to a slave or to a seaman, but to a black trumpeter in the household of Henry VII and Henry VIII. There is an entry in the accounts of the Treasurer of the Chamber dated 7 December 1507 of the payment of twenty shillings for 'John Blanke, the blacke trumpet, for his moneth wages of Novembre last passed at viii d the day' (E 36/214). He may even be the black trumpeter that appears on the illustrated Westminster

Tournament Roll of 1511 (College of Arms Ms: MM. 4 and 28), held to celebrate the birth of a short-lived son to Queen Katherine. A facsimile reproduction of this is available in the PRO Library.

In 1596 Elizabeth I ordered that black people should be sent abroad and in 1601 a proclamation was issued stating that 'the great number of Negroes and Blackamoors which (as she is informed) are crept into this realm' should be 'with all speed avoided and discharged out of this her majesty's dominions' (*Acts of the Privy Council*, xxvi, 1596–7, 16, 20 and 21). In practice such measures proved ineffective and the numbers of Africans continued to grow in the seventeenth and eighteenth centuries.

There were two overlapping groups – the slaves and the free black community. The free community grew up in the ports of London, Liverpool and Bristol where there were communities of sailors and former slaves and their descendants. Planters and merchants brought back slaves from their plantations to become domestic servants. They might in time have gained their freedom, or they might have run away and lost themselves in London or the large ports. It is not always easy to trace people of colour among the records as one is normally dependent on them being designated as such. It is possible to find occasional references among the State Papers (SP), and parish registers (held locally) should always be consulted.

Wills proved in the Prerogative Court of Canterbury (PROB), the Prerogative Court of York (held at the Borthwick Institute – *see* Appendix 4 for address) and in the diocesan courts (diocesan/county record offices) of the aristocracy, gentry and merchant classes can yield information on servants and former slaves. Many middle class households in the eighteenth century might have employed a black servant. An example of this is Dr Samuel Johnson's employment of Francis Barber, who became the chief beneficiary under Johnson's will (PROB 1/19). Estate papers of families connected with the slave trade and the West Indies should also be researched. For this, use the National Register of Archives database, available in the Research Enquiries Room.

6.3.1 Committee for the Relief of the Black Poor, 1786

Records of the Committee for the Relief of the Black Poor 1786 are to be found in T 1: Treasury Board Papers (T 1/631–6, 638, 641–7). These include minutes of the Committee (T 1/631–8 and T 1/641) and Henry Smeathman's plan for the settlement of Sierra Leone (T 1/631/1304). For full references to the relevant Treasury paper numbers *see* PRO RISD Memorandum 567 and Domestic Records leaflet 39.

The scheme was proposed by the committee to solve the problem of poverty among the black community in London. On agreeing to leave the country and live in the new

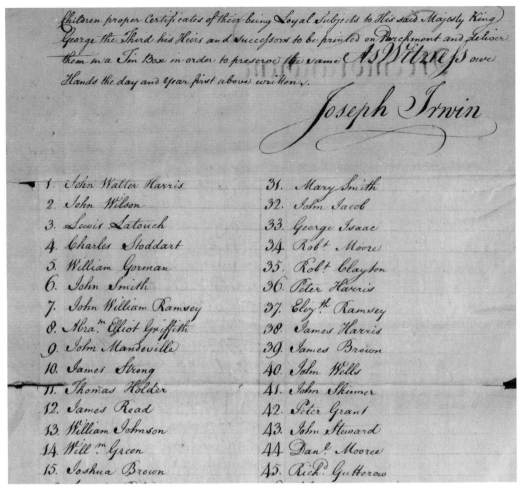

Figure 17 Alphabetical list of the 'Black People who have received the Bounty from Government', 1786: one of two lists of black people who agreed to go and settle in Sierra Leone. Not everyone who signed actually went. Of those that did, most were to perish when the settlement failed (T 1/638 no. 249 p. 2)

settlement in Sierra Leone the volunteers received a bounty payment. Of those who signed the contract to go to Sierra Leone, not everyone actually went, and of those who did, many perished or became slaves or slave traders themselves when the settlement failed shortly after being established.

6.3.2 Seamen's records

Many black men who were not slaves or domestic servants were seamen in the ports. The ship's musters from 1747 and agreements and crew lists from 1835 may be worth consulting. BT 98: Agreements and Crew Lists, Series I are arranged by port up to 1854 and then by ship's official number up to 1860. Unfortunately, only those for Dartmouth, Liverpool, Plymouth and Shields survive before 1800. Only some of the musters include crew names. The agreements and crew lists from 1835 include town or country of birth and other details. Later records are in BT 99: Agreements and Crew Lists, Series II, but these are only a 10 per cent sample for each year. For a guide to these and other records of seamen consult *Records of Merchant Shipping and Seamen* (PRO Readers' Guide No. 20, 1998).

In the Home Office registered file series there is a record HO 144/11017/377969, relating to riots in Cardiff and Liverpool in 1919 involving West Indian and West African seamen. In sub-file 377969/44 are eight lists marked B to I, four of West Indians and four of West Africans, unemployed and employed, unmarried and married. The lists are quite detailed giving name and address, age, country of birth and brief details of how each individual came to be in the United Kingdom. It was proposed to repatriate some of these men under the repatriation of coloured seamen schemes. There are 285 named of which only some 59 were repatriated. The correspondence makes it clear that there had been several hundred black seamen in Liverpool at this time. Many had left the city, going to other towns inland.

6.3.3 Other sources

For advice and guidance on family history contact the Black Genealogical Society (*see* Appendix 4 for address). There is also a useful genealogical web site for those researching ancestry in the West Indies. For records relating to slaves and the abolition of slavery in the West Indies consult *Tracing Your West Indian Ancestors* (PRO Readers' Guide No. 11, 1995). The Black Cultural Archives promotes the collection and documentation of African peoples. Their collections include documentation on the lives and achievements of black people in Britain from the eighteenth to the twentieth centuries.

For information relating to colonial immigration during the twentieth century, *see* Chapter 2.

6.4 German immigrants

There has been a German presence in London since the twelfth century. The merchants of the Hanseatic League were granted privileges in the city, and the Steelyard became the centre of an important community that elected its own aldermen.

Other German merchants had connections with the ports of the east coast, Ipswich, Yarmouth, King's Lynn, Boston, Hull and Newcastle. The Reformation brought new waves of Protestant immigrants to England in the sixteenth and seventeenth centuries – *see* Sections 7.1 and 8.3.

The PRO holds a collection of registers from German Lutheran chapels in London. These can be found in RG 4 as listed below.

German Lutheran chapel registers in the PRO

Chapel	Registers	PRO reference
Hamburg or German Lutheran Chapel, Gt Trinity Lane, City of London	Baptisms 1669–1836, marriages 1671–1754, burials 1695–1836	RG 4/4650
German Lutheran Church, Savoy, Strand	Births and baptisms 1694–1840, marriages 1695–1754, deaths and burials 1722–1840	RG 4/4625–7, 4632 RG 4/4625 RG 4/4628–31
St George's German Lutheran Church, Little Allie Street, Goodmans Fields	Baptisms 1763–1857, burials 1763–1853	RG 4/4543, 4570–71, 4603 RG 4/4544, 4572–3, 4604

These registers can be consulted on microfilm at the Family Records Centre or in the Microfilm Reading Room at Kew. For the German Lutheran Royal Chapel *see* Section 8.4.

The London Metropolitan Archives has records of the German Hamburg Lutheran Church (LMA ref: ACC/2622) and of other German churches (*see* LMA Information Leaflet No. 17, *The German Community in London*). The Anglo-German Family History Society has produced microfiche indexes to St George's German Lutheran Church records (copies available at the FRC and the LMA). *See* Appendix 4 for addresses of these archives.

6.5 Twentieth century communities

The PRO holds no records of ethnic groups who have settled in Britain since the Second World War. Readers are advised to contact social and cultural organizations of these communities – *see* Appendix 4 for useful addresses. Policy files on immigration and nationality will be found among the records of the Home Office – *see* Chapter 3. For records relating to immigration in the twentieth century from the Colonies and New Commonwealth *see* Chapter 2. For records of naturalization *see* Chapter 5.

7 Huguenots and other refugee groups

7.1 The Reformation and religious refugees

The sixteenth century saw the Reformation in Germany and the influx of Protestant refugees at first small in number, and until Henry VIII's break with Rome not particularly welcome. Politically, aliens were a menace to the realm, especially when diplomatic relations with other powers were strained or when war broke out. In one area, however, immigration was encouraged. Henry VIII positively encouraged certain groups of skilled labourers such as ordnance workers, gunners and armourers from France, Germany and the Low Countries, to settle in England. Mathematical practitioners, instrument makers and surveyors were encouraged to enter the King's employment and many of these were made denizens for this purpose – for definition *see* Section 5.1.2.

Other immigrants followed, such as Dutch tapestry-makers, Flemish weavers and glaziers from France and the Low Countries. They often settled in the liberties and precincts of the monasteries where they had freedom from the jurisdiction of the city authorities. The growing numbers led to an Act in 1523 (14/15 Hen. VIII c. 2), regulating stranger craftsmen and a further Act of 1529 (21 Hen. VIII c. 16) to control their activities and regulate their relationship with the city companies. A third Act of 1540 (32 Hen. VIII c. 16) strengthened the law relating to stranger denizens and patents of denization. Following this legislation many of the foreign workmen settled in England took oaths of loyalty as required by the Act of 1529 and paid the necessary fees to obtain patents of denization.

In 1550 Edward VI granted by letters patent the use of the former Austin Friars Church to the German refugees and other strangers. A Pole, John a'Lasco, was to be their superintendent. Initially the church was used by German, Dutch and French congregations. The congregation was dispersed during the reign of Mary, but was restored after Elizabeth came to the throne, under the care of the Bishop of London. The Walloons and French-speaking congregation obtained the lease of St Anthony's Church in Threadneedle Street.

Other communities opened their own churches. One of the earliest nonconformist congregations in England was a foreign community of Walloons in Southampton. A register of baptisms survives in the PRO from 1567 (RG 4/4600). In 1567,

Southampton was willing to admit Dutch settlers who had fled persecution in their own country (SP 12/43 no. 16, f. 41). Protestants from the Low Countries had petitioned the Queen to be allowed to settle in England and carry on their occupations (SP 12/43 no. 29, ff. 66v–68v). The harsh rule of Spain in The Netherlands led to an increase in Flemish and Dutch immigration into England.

7.2 The Huguenots

The Huguenots were French Protestant refugees, who began to flee to England from the mid-sixteenth century onwards, especially after the massacre of St Bartholomew's Eve in 1572 and until the issuing of the Edict of Nantes in 1598 granted them toleration in France. With its revocation in 1685, large numbers of Huguenots again fled and settled in England. Their main settlements were in London, Norwich, Canterbury, Southampton, Rye, Sandwich, Colchester, Bristol and Plymouth. Many records and studies of the Huguenots have been published by the Huguenot Society of London (now the Huguenot Society of Great Britain – *see* Appendix 4 for the address of the Huguenot Library).

7.2.1 State Papers and Privy Council records

State Papers should be consulted for material on the Huguenots, particularly SP 12: State Papers Domestic, Elizabeth I, and later SP 31: State Papers Domestic, James II and SP 32: State Papers Domestic, William and Mary. These are calendared in the *Calendar of State Papers, Domestic Series*. SP 44 State Papers: Entry Books contains applications for denization, including many for French Protestants. (SP 44/67, in particular, covers the period 1678 to 1688.)

PC 2: Privy Council: Registers contains minutes of proceedings, orders, reports, etc. The volumes are fully indexed and Huguenots should be looked for under French Protestants. From 1670 onwards it is also worth consulting PC 4: Minutes and Associated Papers.

7.2.2 Naturalization of foreign Protestants

Under a statute of 1708 for the Naturalization of Foreign Protestants (7 Anne c. 5) all Protestant refugees who took the oaths of allegiance and supremacy in a court of law, and who could produce a sacrament certificate, were deemed to have been naturalized, without the need for individual Acts of parliament. E 169/86 is the oath roll for oaths taken by aliens in the court of the Exchequer from 1709 to 1711. Copies of the sacrament certificates of those naturalized under the statute are in E 196/10. This

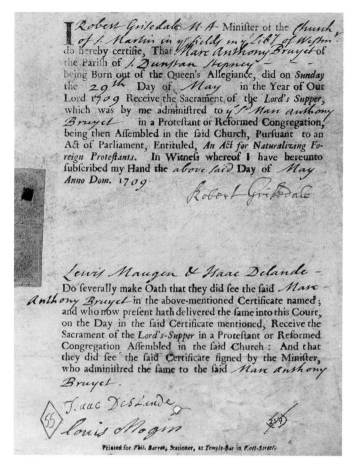

Figure 18 Sacrament certificate of Marc Anthony Bruyet of the parish of St Dunstan's Stepney, signed by the minister of St Martins in the Fields and two witnesses, 29 May 1709 (E 196/10 no. 55)

has been published by the Huguenot Society, vol. xxxv (1932), pp 11–33.

KB 24/2 contains oaths of allegiance and supremacy taken by persons becoming naturalized under the 1708 Act in the court of King's Bench. These have also been published by the Huguenot Society, vol. xxvii (1923), pp. 72–107. This is described in the class list as a naturalization roll (and a duplicate) covering the law terms Easter 1709 to Hilary 1712. Sacrament certificates presented at the court of Chancery may be found in C 224, but there are gaps. Oaths taken locally at Quarter Sessions should be looked for locally among Quarter Sessions records in county record offices – *see* Appendix 2. *See* Chapter 5 for further information on citizenship records.

7.2.3 Registers of foreign Protestant churches

RG 4: Registers of Births, Marriages and Deaths surrendered to the Non-parochial Registers Commissions of 1837 and 1857 contains, among others, registers of the Walloon and French Protestant churches in England and also registers of the Dutch,

German and French Chapels Royal at St James's Palace (*see* Chapter 8). These records are available on microfilm at the Family Records Centre and at the PRO, Kew.

Walloon and French Protestant churches, records in the PRO

Church	Records	PRO reference
Berwick Street Chapel	Births and baptisms 1720–88	RG 4/5484
Canterbury, The Malt House	Births, baptisms and marriages 1709–44	RG 4/4647
Canterbury, Walloon Church (Walloon and French)	Baptisms 1581–1837, marriages 1581–1747, deaths 1590–1715	RG 4/4542, 4564, 4597–9 4601, 4620–22
Castle Street Chapel, Leicester Square	Births, baptisms and marriages 1725–54	RG 4/4549
Crown Street (later Little Edward Street) Les Grecs	Baptisms 1703–31	RG 4/4644
Glasshouse Street Chapel	Births, baptisms and marriages 1688–99	RG 4/4581
Hoxton	Baptisms and marriages 1748–83	RG 4/4559
Hungerford Chapel, Hungerford Market	Births, baptisms and marriages 1688–1727	RG 4/4550
Le Tabernacle	Births, baptisms and marriages 1696–1710	RG 4/4547
Leicester Fields Chapel	Births, baptisms and marriages 1699–1793	RG 4/4582–5
Little Dean Street, Le Quarré	Births, baptisms and marriages 1690–1763	RG 4/4545–6
Newport Market, La Charenton	Births, baptisms and marriages 1701–4	RG 4/4610
Norwich (Walloon and French)	Baptisms 1595–1752, marriages 1599–1611	RG 4/4649
Plymouth, Devon	Baptisms, marriages, burials 1733–1807	RG 4/4623
Plymouth, Stonehouse	Baptisms 1692–1791, marriages 1692–1740, burials 1692–1710, 1743–58, 1762–82.	RG 4/4565–7, 4577
Soho, West Street Chapel	Births and baptisms 1706–43	RG 4/4551
Southampton, Church of St Julian (Walloon and French)	Baptisms 1567–1779, marriages 1567–1753, burials 1567–1722	RG 4/4600
Spitalfields, Eglise de Crispin Street	Baptisms 1694–1716, marriages 1699–1716	RG 4/4562–3
Spitalfields, Eglise de la Patente, Brown's Lane	Baptisms 1689–1785, marriages 1689–1759	RG 4/4596, 4602, 4614–16
Spitalfields, Eglise de l'Artillerie, Artillery Street	Baptisms 1691–1786, marriages 1691–1754, banns 1713–33	RG 4/4560, 4576, 4593–4, 4612
Spitalfields, Eglise de St Jean, St John Street	Baptisms 1691–1786, marriages 1691–1754	RG 4/4578–80, 4590–92, 4635–6
Spitalfields, Eglise de Swan Fields	Baptisms and marriages 1721–35	RG 4/4648
Spitalfields, Eglise de Wheeler Street	Baptisms and marriages 1703–41	RG 4/4561, 4595, 4606, 4613

Church	Records	PRO reference
Spitalfields, Eglise Neuve, Church Street	Baptisms 1753–1809	RG 4/4589
Spitalfields, Threadneedle Street, and Hospital Chapel (Walloon and French)	Baptisms 1599–1840, marriages 1599–1753 and banns 1694–1753	RG4/4552–8, 4587–8, 4634, 4643, 4645–6
St Martin Orgars, Martin Lane, Cannon Street (Walloon)	Births and baptisms 1690–1762, marriages 1698–1751	RG 4/4586
Strand, French Chapel, Savoy	Baptisms 1731–1822, marriages 1684–1753	RG 4/4611, 4641–2
Swallow Street Chapel	Births, baptisms and marriages 1690–1709	RG 4/4609
Thorpe-le-Soken, Essex Eglise de Thorpe-le-Soken	Baptism, marriages and burials 1684–1726	RG 4/4624
Westminster, St Anns Ryder's Court Chapel	Births, baptisms and marriages 1700–50	RG 4/4607–4608

Registers of baptisms at various chapels (RG 4/4637)
Repertorie General

La Patente	1689–1716
Crispin Street	1689–1775
Perle Street	1694–1715
Wheeler Street	1700–1701
Bell Lane	1703–42
Eglise de Marche	1711–16
Brown's Lane	1719–38

The above records can be consulted at the Family Records Centre or in the Microfilm Reading Room at Kew.

7.2.4 The French Committee

The PRO does not hold these records. National collections had been made for the refugees in 1681, 1686, 1688 and 1694. Additional money was given by the Crown and later parliamentary grants. The French Committee administered these grants of money for the relief of French refugees. Surviving records of this body are held by the Huguenot Library, University College, London – *see* Appendix 4 for address.

The French Protestant Church of London has its own library and holds its own registers and other records. The London Metropolitan Archives has a collection of Huguenot Society publications (LMA Information Leaflet No. 24) and collections of material on Huguenot businesses and individuals. *See* Appendix 4 for addresses to these archives.

7.3 Palatinate refugees

In 1709 large numbers of German refugees from the Rhineland Palatinate and south-west Germany found a temporary home in London. Most were planning to settle as colonists in North America, but some abandoned this idea and settled in Ireland, in Limerick and Kerry subsidized by the Irish government. Some settled in the Scilly Isles, and others found employment in the coal mines of the north of England. Lists of some of these refugees arriving in London can be found in T 1/119 giving names of individuals and the number of dependants.

7.4 French émigrés 1789–1815

An influx of French refugees between 1789 and 1814, as a result of the revolution and Napoleonic wars, produced much government concern and documentation, resulting in the Aliens Act 1793 (*see* Section 4.1.1). T 50: Treasury: Pay Lists and other Documents concerning Refugees contains some material on French ships and expenses of refugees (T 50/57–75).

7.4.1 Bouillon Papers

HO 69: Bouillon Papers is a collection of papers and letters to Philippe d'Auvergne, Prince de Bouillon as 'Administrateur des Secours Accordes aux Emigres'. From 1794 to 1815 Bouillon served as the senior naval officer in Jersey defending the Channel Islands, gathering intelligence and supporting French royalist refugees who had fled to Jersey. He was aided by the British government, which provided money for the support of the refugees. The most relevant papers relating to émigrés are in HO 69/33–8.

Other papers of the Prince de Bouillon concerning military matters and the defence of the Channel Islands can be found in this class and in FO 95 and WO 1. There are two registers of refugees in Jersey dated 1793 to 1796 (FO 95/602–603). Privy Council records also contain some of his papers (PC 1/115–22, 134–5 and 4490–516). A detailed list of these papers can be found in the non-standard finding aids, which are arranged in class order on the open shelves in the Research Enquiries Room.

7.4.2 Calonne Papers

Charles Alexandre de Calonne was Controller General of France 1783–7, before living in exile in England from 1787 to 1790 and 1793 to 1802. After his death his papers were seized by the British government, which subsequently purchased them from his son.

These papers mainly relate to commercial and political matters and can be found in Foreign Office (FO 95/630–53) and Privy Council records (PC 1/123–33 and 4517). A detailed list can be found with the Bouillon list in the non-standard finding aids.

7.4.3 *French Refugee and Relief Committee*

The Treasury set up the French Refugee and Relief Committee in 1792. Its records are in the class T 93: French Refugee and Relief Committee: Records covering the period 1792 to 1823. They contain lists of names of those receiving pensions. There are accounts, letter books, memorials and pension lists for the relief of laity and clergy. The class also includes accounts and vouchers for French Protestant refugees from 1813 to 1828. Account books relating to this fund for Protestants for the years 1794 to 1836 are in the British Library (ref. Egerton Mss. 2728–2832) – *see* Appendix 4 for address.

7.5 Nineteenth century refugees

7.5.1 *Polish refugees*

Allowances paid to Polish refugees can be found in the class PMG 53: Allowances to Polish Refugees and Distressed Spaniards (PMG 53/2–8). The registers are individually indexed and cover the period 1860 to 1899. The allowances ceased on the death of the last surviving Polish pensioner in 1899. There are also pay lists for the Poles from 1841 to 1856 (T50/81–97).

7.5.2 *Spanish refugees*

PMG 53: Paymaster General's Office: Allowances to Polish Refugees and Distressed Spaniards contains indexed registers of allowances to Spaniards (PMG 53/1–9) from 1855 to 1909. The allowances ceased on the death of the last Spanish pensioner in 1909.

7.5.3 *Russian and Polish Jews*

For records relating to the Russian and Polish Jews who fled the pogroms in the Russian Empire *see* Section 6.2.2.

8 Immigrants and aliens before 1800

8.1 Alien merchants and immigrants in the medieval period

The foreign community in England during the medieval period came into being through the growth of trade between England and her neighbours. From Roman times, London had been a trading and commercial centre attracting foreign merchants and craftsmen. In the wake of the Normans came a flood of merchants from Normandy and Flanders. In 1157, Henry II allowed the merchants of Cologne to have a guildhall in London and granted them his protection and a number of privileges. During the thirteenth century Italian merchants began to play an important part in the commercial life of the country and in particular of London. The Statute of Merchants passed by the king and council at Acton Burnell in 1283 and amended in 1285 simplified and speeded up the procedure in actions of debt and was of benefit to foreign merchants.

The development of trade in the fourteenth century resulted in aliens becoming some of the most important merchants in England. The policy of Edward III and Richard II was one of encouraging trade by granting alien merchants the freedom to trade. Some records of the Italian bankers to the Crown can be found in C 47: Chancery Miscellanea. In 1350 Edward III had set aside the privileges of London and other boroughs so that all merchants of friendly countries could sell their wares freely, wholesale or retail, in spite of franchises (Parliament Rolls or *Rotuli Parliamentorum ii.232*). This appears to have been a temporary measure, possibly as a result of the Black Death and London soon regained its privileges. In 1378 a proclamation was made that foreign merchants could come to England under the king's protection and trade wholesale and retail in victuals, spices, fruit, furs and all kinds of small goods (*Rot. Parl. iii.47*). They were restricted to dealing wholesale in wine and great merchandise, such as cloth and linen, retail dealing in such goods being reserved to the native burgesses of the towns and the gilds merchant.

Aliens could petition the Crown for denization by letters patent (*see* Section 5.3.2), but few aliens went through the formalities of denization for in matters of personal protection, contract and title to leasehold property, the law courts gave them as much protection as the king's native subjects. Those who had the means to find sponsors could be admitted to the freedom of boroughs, so only in the matter of taxes, the inheritance of property and the holding of public office were they disadvantaged. London and its suburbs had the highest number of aliens followed by Bristol and the coastal areas, but aliens could be found throughout the country, whether craftsmen in the boroughs, household servants or itinerant labourers.

8.1.1 Taxation and customs records

8.1.1.1 Alien subsidies

Inquests, assessments and accounts survive in E 179: Exchequer: King's Remembrancer: Particulars of Account and other records relating to Lay and Clerical Taxation for alien subsidies, although the returns are most numerous for 1440 and 1483–4. The value of the returns is limited as there was widespread evasion and the tax was difficult to collect. Exemptions could be granted and children and clergy were always exempt. The Irish were not held liable after 1442 and certain groups of foreign merchants were exempted in 1483 and 1487. The alien subsidy ceased to be granted as a separate tax in 1512 but the tax on aliens was included in the grants of lay subsidies made in the sixteenth and early seventeen centuries.

The E 179 class lists are arranged by (pre-1974) county, for England and Wales, with separate sections for the Cinque Ports, members of the Royal Household (both courtiers and officials) and Divers, Miscellaneous and Unknown Counties. There are separate lists for taxes paid by clergy, arranged by diocese and those paid by non-clergy (lay subsidies). Only those documents which are described in the lists as including *names* actually list the names of tax-payers. Within the county, they are arranged chronologically by regnal year of the reigning monarch and by administrative sub-divisions of the county known as hundreds, or in some areas, e.g. Yorkshire as wapentakes. Years can be converted into calendar years using C. R. Cheney's *Handbook of Dates* which is on open access. If you do not know in what sub-division of the county the place you are interested in was located, you can find this out from Lewis's, *Topographical Dictionaries of England and Wales*, which is also on open access.

The E 179 database has been developed by the PRO and the University of Cambridge. The database forms the primary means of searching the class of records known as E 179, King's Remembrancer, particulars of account and other records relating to lay and clerical taxation. Only the records relating to lay taxation are available on this database. The class is arranged by county and to date only the records relating to the following counties have been completed: Bedfordshire, Buckinghamshire, Cambridgeshire, Derbyshire, Essex, Hertfordshire, Huntingdonshire, Leicestershire, Lincolnshire, Kent, Northamptonshire, Nottinghamshire, Rutland, Staffordshire, Surrey, Sussex, Warwickshire and the Cinque Ports. Work is underway on the remaining counties. Readers can search the database by places occurring in the documents, the grants of taxation to which documents relate, dates of document and types of document. Each piece in E 179 has a database record which explains the administrative purpose for which the document was created, the date of the document, the taxes it relates to, and a repertory of the place-names that occur in that document. The names of individuals who are taxed in these documents are not recorded on the database.

The alien subsidy came into being in the fifteenth century. In 1440 parliament passed an act which imposed a subsidy on all aliens for three years. This subsidy was a poll tax levied at two rates, 16d per annum on alien householders and 6d per annum on non-householders. Welshmen were exempt as were some denizens, those under twelve years old and members of religious orders. The subsidy was extended by a further act of 1442 for two years, and exemptions were broadened to include the Irish and Channel Islanders.

Inquests were held before the JPs in each county and borough to record all aliens living in each area and returns were sent to the Exchequer. Commissions for the collection of the money were sent out and it was collected and accounted to the Exchequer. A file of commissions and inquests held in various counties is in E 179/270/31. The surviving returns for the collections of 1440 have been analysed in S. J. Thrupp, 'A survey of the alien population of England in 1440', *Speculum*, XXXII (1957), pp. 262–73. The counties with the highest quotas were Hampshire, Kent, Gloucestershire and Yorkshire. The returns for Southwark (E 179/184/212) are calendared in J. L. Bolton, *The Alien Communities of London in the Fifteenth Century: the Subsidy Rolls of 1440 and 1483–4* (Paul Watkins, Stamford, 1998).

In 1449, two new categories of alien taxpayer were created. Alien merchants (Venetians, Italians, Genoans, Florentines, Milanese, Luccans, Cateloners, Albertines, Lombards, Hansers and Prussians) were required to pay 6s 8d per annum and the clerks of alien merchants were to pay 20d per annum. Merchants remaining in the country for longer than six weeks were liable to pay. New exemptions were those aliens born under the king's allegiance in Normandy, Gascony and Guienne.

A new subsidy was granted in 1453 and levied regularly until 1471. The basic tax of 16d for householders and 6d for non-householders remained unchanged, but the rate for alien merchants, brokers, factors and their attorneys was heavily increased to 40s for householders and 20s for non-householders. The last two subsidies were granted in 1483 and 1487 together with an addition of a category of aliens keeping brewing houses. However, Spanish, Breton and German merchants were exempt and Venetians, Genoans, Florentines and Luccans were later exempted from the tax. The Alien Subsidy Roll for London for 1483 (E 179/242/25) and the Alien Subsidy Rolls for Middlesex for 1484 (E 179/141/94, 95) have been calendared in Bolton (*op. cit.*).

The lay subsidies taxed aliens at double the rates of the native population and they were also charged a poll tax. In the poll tax subsidies of 1512, 1514 and 1515, aliens paid double rates on their landed income or goods and a double poll tax, if they had no taxable possessions. Only in 1535–6 and 1546–7 were aliens without taxable land or goods free from paying a poll tax. The subsidy of 1546–7 and a relief of 1549 were the

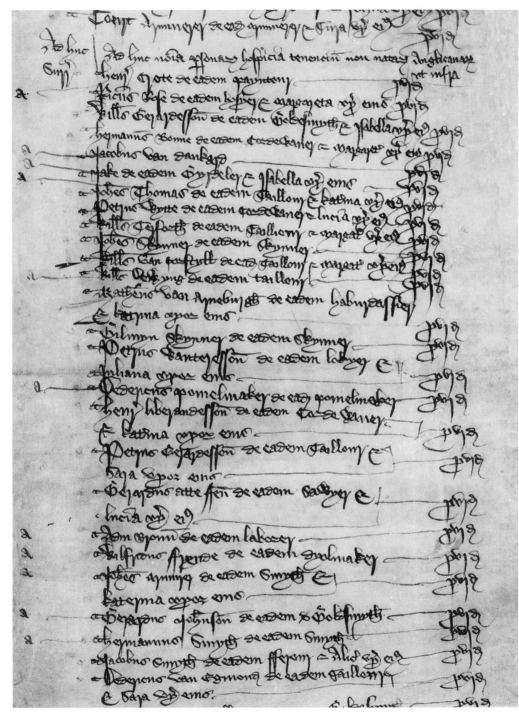

Figure 19 Part of the Surrey and Sussex Alien Subsidy Roll for Southwark 1440 showing householders (E 179/184/212 m. 9v)

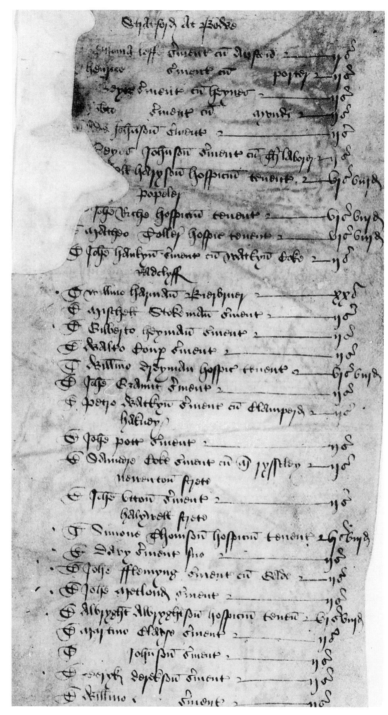

Figure 20 Part of the Middlesex Alien Subsidy Roll for 1484 showing Stratford at Bow, Poplar, etc. (E 179/141/94 m. 4v)

only two subsidies where foreigners were liable to pay at the same rate as native subjects. In 1589 it was ordered that aliens who avoided assessment by putting their property into the hands of their children, would be punished by a double assessment.

8.1.1.2 Customs

In 1290 the citizens of London complained to the king that alien merchants were enriching themselves at their expense. In need of money for his Scottish campaign, Edward I made an agreement with foreign merchants whereby in exchange for his protection and their exemption from a number of local restrictions they would pay a higher rate of customs. This agreement was enacted in the Merchant Charter of 1303. It imposed on foreign merchants the New or Petty Custom, which required them to pay fifty per cent more duty on top of the Ancient Custom imposed on all Staple goods. The custom was extended to imported cloth from 1347 and was payable by both aliens and denizens.

The Exchequer sent out instructions for the customs officers of each port to enter the record of dues collected for each port. The surviving account rolls are to be found in the E 122: Particulars of Customs' Accounts. These record: the names of ships using the port; the name of the masters; dates of arrival or departure and the names of the merchants in whose names the goods were shipped (annotated to denote whether denizen, alien or Hanse); each item of customable cargo, often with its value; and, in the case of the collectors' accounts, the amount payable. This class also contains Exchequer type rolls drawn up after the audit of the accounts and before their enrolment. Accounts which survive in this form often give less information than the rolls of particulars. The list of E 122 is arranged by port, and then by date of account: see the introductory note to the class for more information. Some of these accounts have been printed: E. M. Carus-Wilson (ed.), *The Overseas Trade of Bristol in the Later Middle Ages*, British Record Society, VII (1937); D. M. Daren (ed.), *The Making of King's Lynn: A Documentary Survey*, British Academy, Records of Social and Economic History, IX (1984); W. Childs (ed.), *The Customs' Accounts of Hull 1453–1490*, Yorkshire Archaeological Society 144 (1986); H. S. Cobb (ed.), *The Overseas Trade of London 1480–1*, London Record Society (1990).

The enrolled accounts on the E 372: Pipe Rolls and the E 352: Chancellor's Rolls and from 1323 the E 356: Enrolled Customs' Accounts do not name individual merchants unless they were exempt from payment. The Exchequer Memoranda Rolls (E 159 and E 368) include cases of merchants who attempted to defraud the customs revenue.

Later records of duties paid at particular ports are in the E 190: Port Books from 1565 to 1799. Many books are in poor condition and some do not survive. There are no books for London between 1697 and 1799. The Board of Customs introduced registers of imports and exports from 1696, which effectively superseded Port Books and many ports ceased sending them into the Exchequer in the eighteenth century. A number of Exchequer Port Books have been published by local record societies (*see* E. L. C. Mullins's *Texts and*

Calendars, 2 vols. Royal Historical Society, 1958, 1983). Before 1600 many entries in the Port Books are in Latin – by 1660 most are in English. Lesser ports (in 16th-century terms), sometimes known as 'creeks' or 'havens', were grouped together under 'head ports', thus the returns for Liverpool, Beaumaris and Conway are found with those of the head port of Chester. All are indexed on pp. 564–6 of the E 190 class list.

Separate books were used to record overseas trade and internal coastal trade. Those listed as 'Overseas' record both imports and exports. Those listed as 'Overseas Outwards' record exports only. There are also different series created by different customs officials – the Collector or 'Customer' who had to make a return of all goods exported or imported and all monies received, for which he issued a cocket (receipt); the Controller who had to make a similar return but did not receive the payments; and the Searcher, appointed to prevent fraud, who had to make an independent return based on his examination of the goods and also return a warrant that he had done so. Exchequer officials could then check these returns, warrants and cockets against one another. Entries normally include: the date on which duty was paid, rather than the date of arrival or unloading; the name, tonnage and home port of the ship; the name of the ship's master; the ship's destination or port to which it was sailing next (false information was sometimes supplied, for example, if a merchant was infringing the rights of a monopoly trading company); the names of the merchants (sometimes giving the merchant's mark) and whether they were aliens (aliens paid 25 per cent higher duty); the cargoes they were shipping and the amount of duty paid, based on the official valuation as laid down in the Book of Rates. The spelling of the names of foreign masters or merchants, given verbally, might be taken down wrongly or anglicized. Merchants and masters are described as either natives (*indigent*, often abbreviated to *Ind*) or aliens (*alienigena*, often abbreviated to *Al*).

8.1.1.3 Alien priories

Alien priories were small cells of foreign religious houses that had been established in England. Most had their origin in gifts of land made by Norman landholders in the late eleventh century. A few houses elected their own priors and applied their revenues to their own use, but most were dependent on their mother houses, who appointed and removed their priors at will and received all their revenues. In many cases the priories were small cells of only two or three monks. During the Hundred Years War between England and France these lands and possessions were seized by the crown and placed in the hands of royal keepers. They were normally returned when peace was restored. The revenues of the alien priories were used by the crown to pay for the war and reward loyal service. As a result, these priories suffered financial difficulties and many bought charters of denization from the crown, becoming dependencies of English houses instead. Some ninety priories that had not sought denization were seized by Henry V in 1414 and their estates became crown property. These lands were often appropriated for new religious and educational foundations.

The records concerned with the administration and management of these lands, possessions and revenues were kept by the King's Remembrancer and form the class E 106: Exchequer: King's Remembrancer: Extents of Alien Priories, Aliens, etc. They include Extents and Inquisitions listing the lands and possessions of aliens and alien priories, and indentures recording the return of property. There are also lists of fines and subsidies from aliens and alien clergy recording the payments they made to the crown. Inquisitions concerning the debts of aliens and alien priories and receipts for payments received by royal servants from the keepers or farmers of the lands, are also listed. There are also various writs, a few certificates of mainprise (undertakings to pay specific sums into the Exchequer) and some other miscellaneous documents. The documents range from 1293 to 1483 and there is an index of alien priories and place names (but not of individuals) at the beginning of the class list.

8.2 The medieval Jewish community

The Jewish community had a presence in England from the Norman Conquest, when they came over in the wake of William the Conqueror, until Edward I expelled them in 1290. Henry I granted the Jews a number of privileges. A Jew could acquit himself in a court of law if he found one Jew and one Christian to testify to his innocence, or, if he could find no witnesses, by swearing on a scroll of the Hebrew Pentateuch. Jurisdiction in cases involving Jews were reserved to royal courts or to the constables of royal castles in places where Jews lived. They became in effect royal chattels in return for royal protection. King John confirmed the liberties granted to the Jews by Henry I in 1201 (C 53/4 m. 5). The Jews paid 4,000 marks for the privileges granted by the charter. No line of descent has been established from the members of this early community.

8.2.1 Taxation of Jews

Royal tallages of enormous sums were levied on the Jewish community in the twelfth and thirteenth centuries. A tallage of 1194, the Northampton 'Donum' (E 101/249/2), is a record of the amounts given by the Jewish community towards the 5,000 marks raised by the English Jews for the ransom of Richard I. The Jewish assessment was three times that of the assessment of London. The actual allotment of the sum among the different communities was arranged by the Jews themselves when their representatives met at Northampton in March 1194. The roll lists Jews arranged under towns, giving their names and the amounts contributed. Only about half the amount was actually raised.

The Exchequer of the Jews was established during the reign of Richard I. It was concerned with the collection of tallages and the registration of loans and other financial business. It also acted as a court to settle disputes between Jews and between Jews and Christians. The class of records E 9: Exchequer of the Jews: Plea Rolls

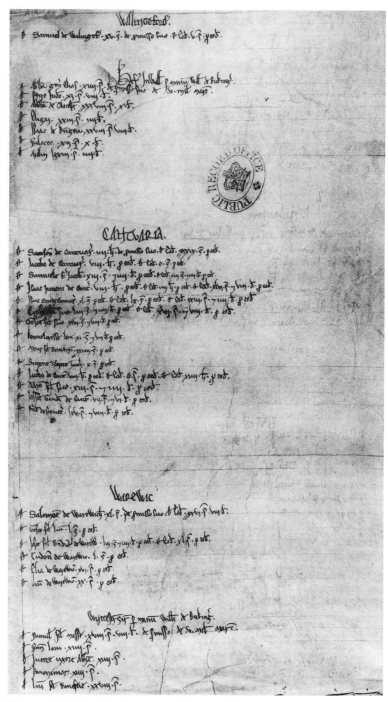

Figure 21   The Northampton 'Donum' 1194: part of the roll showing the Jewish donors and amounts collected in Wallingford, Hereford in Wales, Canterbury and Warwick (E 101/249/2)

contains the surviving plea rolls from 1219 to 1286. Only one roll survives before 1244, however, and only five before 1266. The majority cover the last twenty years of the court's existence. These rolls are being published by the Jewish Historical Society as the *Calendar of the Plea Rolls of the Exchequer of the Jews*, vols 1–5. An analysis of the rolls and their history, by Dr P. A. Brand, will appear in the sixth volume when it is published. None of the writs and returns kept by the court have survived. Some original Jewish bonds are in DL 27: Duchy of Lancaster: Deeds, Series LL, E 40: Exchequer: Treasury of Receipt: Ancient Deeds, Series A, and E 326: Exchequer: Augmentation Office: Ancient Deeds, Series B.

Among the receipt rolls of the Exchequer are a special series of Jewish receipt rolls covering various dates 14 John – 23 Edw. I (E 401/1564–1610), though Jews can also appear on the ordinary rolls. These record the tallages, fines and amercements on the Jewish community. See Hilary Jenkinson, 'The records of Exchequer Receipts from the English Jewry', *Transactions of the Jewish Historical Society of England*, vol. 8. Henry III extended the practice of raising revenue by resorting to arbitrary taxes on the Jews and tallages became a regular source of income for the crown. In 1230 a tallage of 8,000 marks was levied on the Jews and in 1231 a further tallage of 6,000 marks. A tax on the third part of the Jews' moveable property was levied in 1239. In 1241 a tallage of 20,000 marks was levied on the Jews. This tallage was assessed by a gathering of Jews, six from each of the larger communities and two from each of the smaller ones, who met at Worcester the Sunday before Lent. Original receipts of these taxes can be found in E 402: Exchequer of Receipt: Original Receipts.

8.2.2 The expulsion of the Jews

Edward I had a policy of suppressing the practice of usury even by the Jews. Many rich Jews had been impoverished by constant taxation. In 1274 a tallage had been imposed while the king was absent on crusade which was collected by the Knights Templar at the New Temple in London. Those Jews now unable to pay were banished from England. A roll of the receipts from this tallage survives (E 101/249/16). By the *Statutum de Judeismo* of 1275, Jews were forbidden to practice usury and as a result many took to clipping the coinage. A commission was appointed to inquire into coinage offences and on 17 November 1278, Jews were arrested and their houses searched. Many were tried and hanged and the opportunity was taken to enforce the law strictly. Blasphemy against the Christian religion and apostasy by a convert were to be severely punished. Jewish women had to wear a badge of shame, as men had done since the Lateran Council of 1215, and Jews were no longer allowed to employ Christian servants.

The end came in 1290 when orders went out to the sheriffs to seize the *archae*, the chirograph chests containing the sealed bonds and contracts between Jews and Christians. A writ survives to the sheriff of Lincoln to seal and place in safe custody the *archae* of the Jews at Stamford and Lincoln, as do writs to the sheriffs of York and

Gloucester to seize the *archae* at York and Bristol. All deeds not in these chests were to be presented to the Exchequer within the month, i.e. by 16 July 1290, or cease to have validity. Two days after the final date when bonds might be presented, Edward I issued the order expelling the Jews from England (C 54/107 m. 5).

Jews were ordered to leave the country before the Feast of All Saints (1 November). Any who remained after that date were liable to the death penalty. They were allowed to take with them ready money and personal property and any unredeemed pledges of Christians, but bonds and real estate became the property of the Crown. Letters patent were directed to the bailiffs, barons and sailors of the Cinque Ports giving save conduct for Jews leaving the realm with their wives, children and goods (C 66/109 m. 14). The *archae* were brought to London, together with other bonds and obligations and inquisitions were held by the sheriffs into the houses and tenements of the Jews. Much of the property was given to royal favourites. A roll of grants of Jews' houses in various counties, and the synagogues at Oxford, Norwich, Canterbury and Hereford survives in C 67/4 m. 2. A few Jews continued to enter England after the expulsion, but those who lived in the country for any length of time were converts to Christianity.

For later Jewish immigration records *see* Sections 3.4.2 and 6.2.2.

8.3 Aliens and strangers

There are various reports and returns of aliens and 'strangers' among the early State Papers and records of the Privy Council. SP 1: State Papers Henry VIII calendared in *Letters and Papers, Foreign and Domestic, of the Reign of Henry VIII* (copies available in the Map and Large Document Room) should be consulted for political and social policy towards craftsmen and tradesmen, and also for lists of petitioning aliens and strangers. SP 10: State Papers Domestic Edward VI contains a number of returns of aliens between 1547 and 1553.

The authorities were keen to encourage skilled craftsmen into England to establish new trades and industry and many settlements were established around the country. Returns of the numbers of strangers, appear in SP 12: State Papers Domestic Elizabeth I. There is a list dated 22 June 1561 of over 200 men born under the allegiance of the King of Spain who were members of the German Church in London (SP 12/17 no. 33 ff 68–71). It gives details of their families, trades and occupations. There are also some statistical returns which just give numbers only, for example, a certificate of all strangers in London, Westminster and Southwark, dated 20 January 1563 (SP 12/27 no. 19 f 36).

There are some returns, however, for London and surrounding areas that give lists of all those living in the wards and parishes by name. There is one taken in November 1571 (SP 12/82), addressed to Sir William Cecil, of all strangers in London and Southwark, the City and Liberties, and one addressed to the Privy Council of all

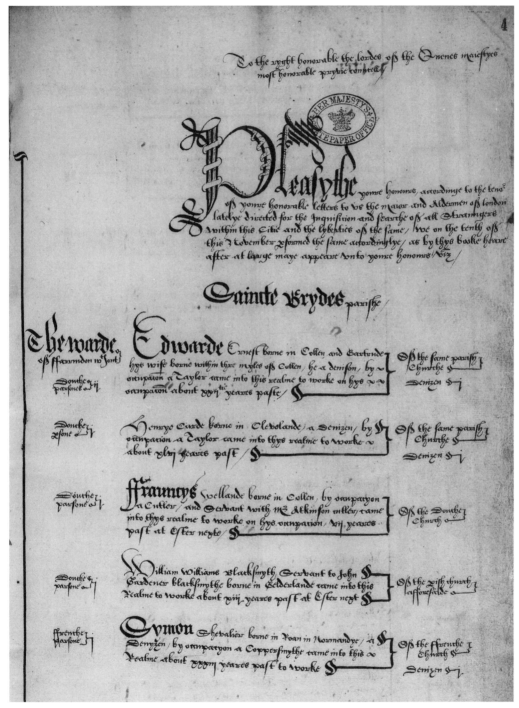

Figure 22 Part of a return addressed to the Privy Council of all strangers in the City and Liberties of London, showing St Brides Parish, 1571 (SP 12/82 f. 4)

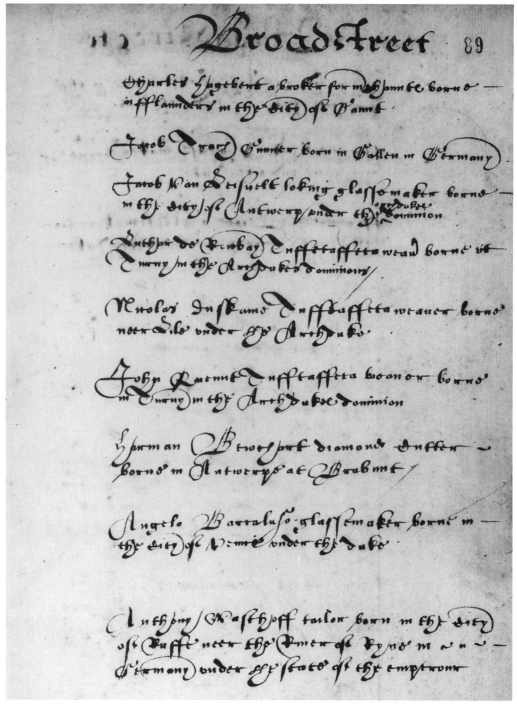

Figure 23 Strangers dwelling in Broadstreet Ward of the City of London in September 1618 (SP 14/102 f. 89)

strangers abiding within the City of London and the Liberties and Suburbs, December 1571 (SP 12/84). There is a later survey by ward of strangers dwelling within London and the Liberties taken about September 1618 (SP 14/102). These have been transcribed and published by the Huguenot Society together with other returns of aliens resident in London (Huguenot Society Publications, vol. X parts I–IV, 1900–08). These returns cover the period from 1523 to 1625 and include lay subsidies, registers of the German or Dutch Church, Austin Friars, State Papers and the Lansdowne Manuscripts in the British Library – *see* Appendix 4 for address.

8.4 Dutch William and German George

The reigns of William III (1689–1702) and George I (1714–27) saw a number of their fellow countrymen come and settle in England. Those that settled usually had connections with the court, government or the army. SP 32: State Papers Domestic William and Mary and SP 35: State Papers Domestic George I should be consulted using the *Calendars of State Papers, Domestic William and Mary* and *Calendars of State Papers Domestic George I* (List and Index Society vols cxxix, cxliv, clv and clxv with indexes in clxxiii). SP 44: State Papers: Entry Books includes passes to pass beyond the sea (SP 44/386–413) covering the period 1697 to 1784. These give the name and sometimes residence of individuals permitted to travel overseas within a prescribed period. They usually give port of departure and destination.

8.4.1 Registers of foreign Chapels Royal

Chapel	Registers	PRO reference
Dutch Chapel Royal, St James's Palace, Westminster	Baptisms and marriages 1689–1740, baptisms 1742–75, marriages 1743–54	RG 4/4574–75
French Royal Chapel, St James's	Births, baptisms and marriage licences 1700–56	RG 4/4640 RG 4/4539–41
German Lutheran Royal Chapel of St James's Palace, Westminster	Baptisms and marriages 1712–20, baptisms 1760–1836	RG 4/4568 RG 4/4569
Whitehall Chapel Royal	Marriage licences 1687–1754, 1807	RG 8/76–8

8.4.2 Lord Chamberlain's records

LC 3: Lord Chamberlain's Department: Various Registers includes establishment books listing officials and servants of the Royal Household. These include a number of Dutch and German subjects. There are also two series of appointments books. Many of these are indexed. There are a few papers relating to appointments for this period. LC 5: Lord Chamberlain's Department: Miscellaneous Records contains warrants for tradesmen with orders for goods, etc. and petitions.

8.4.3 Other records

There are registers of subscribers to loans for 1698 and 1709–10 among the Exchequer of Receipt records (E401/2592, 2594, 2595), which include the names of recent settlers. There is also a register of beneficiaries in a lottery of 1712 (E 401/2599–2160).

T 1: Treasury Papers for this period should also be consulted as it contains the original correspondence with the Treasury. T 4: Books of Applications contains entries of petitions to the Treasury from 1680. The *Calendars of Treasury Papers 1557–1728* and *Calendars of Treasury Books 1660–1718* should be used to find relevant material.

8.5 Russians

RG 8: Registers of Births, Marriages and Deaths Surrendered to the Non-parochial Registers Commission of 1857 contains registers and other records of the Russian Orthodox Church in London from 1721 to 1927 (RG 8/111–304). This church was attached to the Russian Embassy and was used by the embassy staff, but it was also used by the small Russian community in London. The majority of the registers are in Russian, but some are in Greek and a few documents are in French and German.

8.6 Alien estates

C 205: Chancery: Petty Bag Office: Special Commissions of Inquiry is a class of records of commissions to establish the Crown's right to certain property, including lands that were forfeited or could be forfeited to the Crown. Bundles 1–3 relate to aliens including the forfeiture of the lands and property of deceased aliens and of living enemy aliens in wartime. Aliens could acquire moveable property and rent landed property, but in law could not purchase land or dower their wives. Aliens of enemy nations had no rights or privileges except by the monarch's special favour in times of war. There is an index of names at the beginning of the class list and the bundles relating to aliens cover the period from circa 1639 to 1883. There are only some 120 cases in these bundles; some of the dates are conjectural and many are nineteenth century.

Appendix I

Using packing lists

Some PRO classes, such as HO 45 and HO 144, contain documents which have two-part references – a box number and a file or paper number. This is because the vast majority of documents within these classes of records are individual files packed together within boxes. The files are arranged by Home Office paper number. In order to obtain a naturalization file it is necessary to know both the Home Office paper number and the reference number of the box which contains it. A document from these classes cannot be produced without both of these numbers. Essentially, therefore, the document ordering terminal will require the following information:

- group lettercode (e.g. HO)
- class number (e.g. 144)
- piece number (i.e. Box Number/Paper Number).

In order to obtain the full PRO reference for the document you require follow these three steps:

Step one
Identify the Home Office paper number for the naturalization you require from the nominal indexes to naturalizations.

Step two
Then find the number of the box it was packed in by consulting the HO 45 and HO 144 'Packing Lists'. These lists can be found among the series of HO class lists and are arranged internally by grouping years: 1871–8 (HO 45 only); 1879–1900; 1901–19; 1920; 1921–2; with each year noted separately between 1923 and 1950. There are no packing (or box) lists for the period before 1871.

Identify the relevant grouping year within the 'Packing List' for the date of the file and match up the paper number with the box number: the general rule is that memorial paper numbers for naturalizations between 1872 and 1878 will be found in the HO 45 Packing List and papers after 1878 will be found in the HO 144 Packing List. However, this is *not always* the case. It is best to check both if necessary. Similarly, if you cannot find a paper number among what appears to be the correct date (i.e. the period in which naturalization was granted) within the Packing List, check to see whether it has been filed under a later date. This is often the case where a file has had to be re-opened by the Home Office at a later date and was, consequently, filed away at a later date.

Step three
Match your paper number with the box number. You are now equipped with a full PRO document reference.

For example, the full PRO reference for the naturalization papers of Christian Matthes (HO paper number B30868) is: HO 144/451/B30868. The components of this reference are in bold type in the

Table below. HO is the PRO lettercode for Home Office. The class number is 144. The box in which the papers are packed is number 451, and the number of the actual paper is B30868.

	Home Office Packing List, 1879–1900						
HO 144							
Box 451	B30778;	B30779;	B30782;	B30784;	B30785;	B30787;	B30791;
	B30793;	B30796;	B30803;	B30804;	B30824;	B30832;	B30833;
	B30835;	B30842;	B30848;	B30849;	B30853;	B30862;	B30867;
	B30868;	B30869;	B30878;	B30879;	B30880;	B30883;	B30893;
	B30894						

Appendix 2

Immigration records held in county record offices, other local authority record offices and police archives in England and Wales

As well as central government, local councils and local voluntary bodies have also at times been concerned with immigrants. Records relating to immigrants can therefore be found in any of these. Quarter Session records, Poor Law records and school records are examples of sources where details of individual immigrants may survive. These sources may be found in local county record offices, police archives and other local authority record offices. *Restrictions on access to records may vary from archive to archive, and it is advisable to contact any institution before visiting in person.*

In 1999, local repositories kindly responded to the authors' request for specific references to documents relating to immigrants. Although many referred to the inclusion of references in general sources such as Poor Law records, Quarter Sessions records and school records, some provided more detailed references. The findings are listed below. The references given in the third column of the listing are the internal reference numbers of the individual archives.

England

Avon

Bristol Record Office
Smeaton Road
Bristol BS1 6XN

List of aliens among Quarter Sessions papers	1814	JQS/P/313
Register of suspected aliens, with current address if known	1914–59	Pol/Reg/3/1

Bedfordshire

Bedfordshire and Luton Archives and Record Service
County Hall
Cauldwell Street
Bedford MK42 9AP

Aliens' police registration cards	1919–	Po/RA
Various Belgian refugee committee records, letters and reports concerning Henlow, Stevington, and Bedford districts	1915–28	P39/5/1; P71/28/50; Z250/22–31

Buckinghamshire

County Records and Local Studies Service
County Hall
Aylesbury
Bucks HP20 1UU

Posse Comitatus: includes details of males over 15 at the French School (for émigrés) at Penn	1798	L/P 15, 16
List of officials and servants in the households of King Louis XVIII, the Queen and the Duke and Duchess of Angoulême	c. 1808	D 54/44
Reminiscences, photographs and other memorabilia of Italian ex-POWs in Buckinghamshire	1939–45	AR 139/95
Young People from occupied countries – correspondence and photos of 20 Dutch boys sent to Aylesbury while Holland recovered from the war	1946–7	NQ5/23/1

Cambridgeshire

County Record Office Cambridge
Shire Hall
Cambridge CB3 OAP

Cambridgeshire and Swaffham Prior Belgian Hospitality Committee reports and minutes	1917, 1919	P150/24/2–3
Wood Ditton Parish Council details of Belgian refugees	1917	P55/AM/1
Barton church service register of Belgian refugee attendees	1916	P10/1/13
Willingham Parish Council, Committee for Belgian refugees: minutes and papers	1915	P177/AM/7 and P177/AC/19
Great Wilgraham Parish Council, details of accommodation for Belgian refugees	1915	P174/AM/1
Grants made to British-born wives of interned aliens by Cambridgeshire Poor Law Guardians	1914–19	G/C/AX28
Lists of Italians held at Townley Memorial Hall, Fulbourn	1939–45	335/Q18
Refugees from Nazi Germany in Cambridge: minutes of Cambridge Branch of the National Union of Women Workers	1937–49	789/Q4

County Record Office Huntingdon
Grammar School Walk
Huntingdon PE18 6LF

Register of aliens	1914–18	Acc. 4440/95/80
Register of aliens	1939–c. 1960	Acc. 4440/379/90
Register of aliens	1953–4	Acc. 4440/77/90

Cheshire

Cheshire Constabulary
Castle Esplanade
Nuns Road
Chester CH1 2PP

Alien registration cards	1965–

Cumbria

Cumbria Record Office
The Castle
Carlisle CA3 8UR

Refugees: Czech refugees at Hawse End, Derwentwater	1938–42	D/Mar 6/1–13
Alien record cards	1940–	

Cumbria Record Office
County Office
Kendal LA9 4RQ

German prisoners of war at Shap Wells: photograph album	1941–2	WS/CONS/6/6

Derbyshire

Derbyshire Record Office
County Offices
Matlock
Derbyshire DE4 3AG

Belper, Tideswell and Stanley Belgian refugee committee minutes, correspondence and accounts	1914–30	D302 Z/OZ15; D1494 A/PZ 3; D331/1/35–45

Devon

Plymouth and West Devon Record Office
3 Clare Place
Coxside
Plymouth PL4 0JW

Orders for aliens to appear at the Guildhall with passports and licences	1807	Acc. W362/39
Registration papers and passports of aliens	1802–22	Acc. W674

Dorset

Dorset Record Office
Bridport Road
Dorchester DT1 1RP

Dorset alien subsidy roll during William Caraunt's shrievalty of Somerset and Dorset (includes lists for Wells, Bruton, Yeovil, Lamport, and Taunton)	c. Hen VI	D/WLC:X2
Ritson Family papers: correspondence and papers relating to Austrian Jewish refugees	1938–59	D.1507

Essex

Essex Record Office
County Hall
Chelmsford CM1 1LX

Lay subsidy book references	1587–8	D/DP 04
Return of foreigners of All Saints, Maldon	18th c.	D/B 3/3/422/1
Estreats of foreign traders, Maldon	1740–54	D/B 3/3/540
Instructions and investigations of enemy aliens	1914–18	J/P 12/1,6
Aliens registration cards	c. 1900–c. 1980	
Numbers of aliens registered in police districts	1932–42	J/P 3/3

Essex Record Office
Colchester and North East Essex Branch
Stanwell Street
Colchester CO2 7DL

Shaftesbury German prisoner of war camp, Dovercourt: papers	1944–8	D/DU 1147

Gloucestershire

Shire Hall Records Centre
Shire Hall
Westgate Street, Gloucester

Correspondence of the county education department concerning the settlement and education of Hungarian and Polish refugees	c. 1950s	K 482
Receivership files including papers on immigrants from Croatia, Hungary, Ukraine and Yugoslavia	1933–57	K1013
Croatian passports	1944–5	K1013/16

Gloucestershire County Record Office
Clarence Row
Alvin Street
Gloucester GL1 3DW

Refugees from the Nazi regime seeking homes in Gloucester and elsewhere	1939–45	D7501

Hampshire

Hampshire Record Office
Sussex Street
Winchester
Hampshire SO23 8TH

Petition to parliament concerning the suffering of Huguenot refugees living in England	c. 1690	44M69/G2/127
Ourry family papers (Huguenots)	c. 1700s	4M52
Passports issued by the Mayor of Winchester allowing French persons (mainly clergy) to travel within the county	1793–1804	WD/382
Photographs of immigrants at Southampton dock	1953	139M86/263/1–2

Portsmouth Museum and Record Services
Museum Road
Portsmouth PO1 2LJ

Typed list of Polish soldiers who landed at Portsmouth	1834	I/328

Southampton Archives Service
Civic Centre
Southampton SO14 7LY

Aliens property record books 1939–41 SC/P 32/2–3
Southampton Port Health Department 1972–8
   passenger lists

Herefordshire

Hereford Record Office
The Old Barracks
Harold Street
Hereford HR1 2QX

Belgian refugees committee records 1914–19 BH 42/1–13

Hertfordshire

Hertfordshire Archives and Local Studies
County Hall
Hertford SG13 8EJ

Copies of naturalization acts 1748–93 D/EBp F1 and 6191–4
Lists of oaths for the naturalizing of
   foreign Protestants 1709 QSMisc 1145

Kent

Canterbury Cathedral Archives
The Precincts
Canterbury CT1 2EH

French church elders' and deacons' 1576–1836
   accounts, registers of wills and
   marriage contracts

East Kent Archives Centre
Enterprise Business Park
Honeywood Road
Whitfield
Dover CT16 3EH

East Kent Lunatic Asylum/St 1920–60 MH/T3/KZ1
   Augustine's Hospital, Chatham:
   register of alien/Polish/Jewish
   patients
Folkestone borough: scrap albums 1914–18 Fo/Z3/1–2
   containing newscuttings, reports and
   photographs on: the arrest of enemy
   aliens in Folkestone; the anti-alien
   campaign, Belgian soldiers and help for
   refugees; Canadians in Folkestone and at
   Shornecliffe Camp; the arrival of refugees

Medway Archives and Local Studies Centre
Civic Centre
Strood
Rochester ME2 4AU

Composite register, containing baptisms and burials including burials of several French and Dutch prisoners	1783–1804	P 153

Leicestershire

The Record Office for Leicestershire, Leicester and Rutland Record Office
Long Street
Wigston Magma
Leicester LE18 2AH

Belgian refugees committee	1914–18	2'20
Aliens registration certificates	1919–67	DE 5491

Greater London

City of Westminster Archives Centre
10 St Ann's Street
London SW1P 2DE

St Marylebone Borough Council: Belgian refugees committee minutes	1915

Corporation of London Records Office
PO Box 270
Guildhall
London EC2P 2EJ

Accounts of funds collected for the relief of French Protestant refugees	1693–1718

London Borough of Sutton Archives
c/o Central Library
St Nicholas Way
Sutton
Surrey SM1 1EA

Sutton UDC Belgian refugee committee minutes	1914–16	LG13/1/74
Letters of appreciation from Belgian refugees	1915	Acc. 130
Borough of Sutton and Cheam refugee family committee minutes	1959–67	Acc. 16

London Metropolitan Archives
40 Northampton Road
London EC1R OHB

Family Welfare Association: East End Mission to the Jews	1896–1931	A/FWA/C
United Synagogue: alien immigration	1903–21	ACC/2712/15
Horton Hospital: aliens register	1948–70	H22/HT/B/17
Jews' Temporary Shelter: committees	1885–1972	LMA/4184/01
Jews' Temporary Shelter: registers of inmates, shipping register	1896–1998	LMA/4184/03
London County Council: Hungarian children	1957	LCC/CH/M
London County Council: refugees	1956–61	LCC/CL/WEL/1
London County Council: Hungarian refugees and students	1956–61	LCC/EO/HFE/1, 3
Metropolitan Asylums Board: camps	1914–19	MAB
Middlesex County Council: refugees from Channel Islands, Gibraltar and Belgium	1940–45	MCC/WE/PA/2
Middlesex County Council: relief of Hungarian refugees	1956–8	MCC/CH/CO/1
Middlesex County Council: returns of aliens	1797–8	MR/A
Middlesex County Council: refugees	1940	MCC/CL/L/CC/1
Poplar Board of Guardians: relief to families of interned aliens	1914–20	PO/BG/151
Bow Street Magistrates Court: extradition registers	1893–1966	PS/BOW/C/01–02
Shoreditch Board of Guardians: aliens	1914–20	SH/BG
Saint Marylebone Board of Guardians: returns of aliens to Medical Officer of Health	1914–20	STM/BG/223
Wandsworth Board of Guardians: relief for families of aliens	1914–17	WA/BG
Woolwich Board of Guardians: returns of alien families	1914–20	WO/BG

Greater Manchester

Central Library
St Peter's Square
Manchester M2 5PD

List of foreign merchants in Manchester	1781–1870	MS ff 382 S35
List of foreign merchants in Manchester	1784–1845	MS Q 382 S36
Account of weekly payments to Irish poor in Manchester by churchwardens	1809–48	M3/3/6

Greater Manchester Police Museum
Newton Street
Manchester M1 1ES

City of Salford police registers of aliens	1914–60	

Greater Manchester Record Office
56 Marshall Street
New Cross
Manchester M4 5FU

City of Salford police registers of aliens	1914–60	

Salford City Archives Centre
658/662 Liverpool Road
Irlam
Manchester M44 5AD

Belgium refugee committee signed minutes (Irlam Urban District)	1914–15	U8/AM1

Norfolk

Norfolk Constabulary
Martineau Lane
Norwich NR1 2DJ

Nominal index of aliens registration records (incomplete)	1914–61	
Aliens daybook (notification of address), Norwich City Police	1920–47	

Norfolk Record Office
Gildengate House
Anglia Square
Upper Green Lane
Norwich NR3 1AX

Norwich militia and military records with lists of all able-bodied men aged between 16 and 60 (including Dutchmen and Walloons)	1511–1630	Norwich City Records Case 13a
Norwich books of aliens (including orders for Dutch and Walloon Strangers)	1492–1686 (1564–1643)	Norwich City Records Case 17d
Norwich Strangers Book (Dutch and Walloon)	1583–1643	MC 189/1, 634 x 3(a)
St Andrew's Hospital registers of admissions (including Polish airmen) under Emergency Hospital Scheme	1941–7	SAH 343–7

Northamptonshire

Northamptonshire Record Office
Wootton Hall Park
Northampton NN4 8BQ

Alien registration cards issued by Northamptonshire Police Authority	1919–	

Northumberland

Morpeth Records Centre
The Kylins
Loansdean
Morpeth
Northumberland NE61 2EQ

Registration of aliens	1913–34	NC/3/46–8

Nottinghamshire

Nottinghamshire Archives
County House
Castle Meadow Road
Nottingham NG2 1AG

Nottingham: declarations of aliens, licences to remain in England, lists of people not granted licences	1798–1800	CA6010
Nottingham: Belgian Refugees Relief Committee minute book	1914–18	CA/CM 72/1
Letter including information about Belgian refugees in Newark and newspaper cutting re register of refugees	1914	DDH178/141–2
Nottingham: German prisoners treated at the City Hospital	1944–5	CA/TC10/120/25/9
Nottingham: use of German prisoners on construction of buildings and road	1945–7	CA/TC10/121/9/2 & 10/5
Police file on escaped German prisoner of war	1940–57	CC/NP32/2
Welbeck: photographs of German prisoners	1940–45	DD1553/2/2–5

Oxfordshire

Oxfordshire Archives
County Hall
New Road
Oxford OX1 1ND

Education of Poles	1953–60	

Shropshire

Shropshire Records and Research Centre
Castle Gates
Shrewsbury SY1 2AQ

Church Stretton minutes of Belgian refugees sub-committee	1914–17	DA7/119/3
Shrewsbury and Atcham Belgian refugee committee minutes	1915	SABC
Ruyton XI Towns Belgian refugees committee minutes	1914–18	1387/45
Church Stretton Council for European Refugees: minutes of the Haven Refugee hostel	1939–48	186/1–7

Somerset

Archives and Record Office
Bath and North East Somerset Record Office
The Guildhall
High Street
Bath BA1 5AT

Aliens licences	1798	Bath QS

Somerset Record Office
Obridge Road
Taunton TA2 7PU

Chipdale and Raddington Belgian Relief Committee minutes	1914–15	DD/CPL 94
Correspondence relating to Belgian refugees in the Chard area	1916–17	D/B/ch/9/2/2

Staffordshire

Staffordshire Record Office
County Buildings
Eastgate Street
Stafford ST16 2LZ

Register of aliens: Leek division of the Staffordshire Constabulary	1916–46	C/PC/2/23

Suffolk

Suffolk Record Office
Raingate Street
Bury St Edmunds IP33 2AR

Notes on British Augustinian nuns from Bruges temporarily housed at Hengrave Hall near Bury St Edmunds	1794–1802	312/13–18
Papers relating to Ugandan Asians at ex-RAF Stradishall near Haverhill	1972–3	EF 509/1/126

Suffolk Record Office
Gatacre Road
Ipswich IP1 2LQ

Lists of aliens in Suffolk, with trades, etc.	1485	HD11:4291/1/10.28
Notes on Vaudois and French refugees in Ipswich	1689–1705	HD:4291/6.22
Notes on aliens and Huguenots in Ipswich		HD11:4291/13.34

Suffolk Record Office
Clapham Road South
Lowestoft
Suffolk NR32 1DR

Account of the ship *MY Studig* taken into Yarmouth harbour with refugees from Estonia, Latvia and Lithuania	1945	ST 315/4/23

Surrey

Surrey History Centre
130 Goldsworth Road
Woking
Surrey GU21 1ND

Alien registration index cards for Surrey County Constabulary	1948–90	CC654
Weybridge Urban District Council papers concerning the relief of Belgian refugees	1914–19	Acc. 1321/–
Ugandan refugee resettlement camp and school: reports and registers	1972–3	CC26

Sussex

East Sussex County Record Office
The Maltings
Castle Precincts
Lewes
East Sussex BN7 1YT

French refugees in Rye	1569–72	RYE/144/18
Belgian refugees at North Bin (Mayfield)	1915	ACC 5792/4
Register of Aliens (East Sussex Constabulary)	1914–17	SPA 8/2/1

West Sussex Record Office
County Hall
Chichester
West Sussex PO19 1RN

Lists of aliens residing in the Chichester and Steyning police divisions	1923–77	
Worthing refugee committee records	1939–78	Add.Mss.27, 809–87

Tyne and Wear

Tyne and Wear Archives
Blandford Square
Newcastle upon Tyne NE1 4JA

Belgian Refugee Community, Birley, transcripts of parish records	1916	C/B13/23
Tynemouth County Borough, internment of aliens	1940	T15/265
Internment of aliens	1939–42	PA/NC/5/24
Suspect lists	1941–4	PA/NC/5/52
Suspect lists	1944–5	PA/NC/5/53
Sabotage, aliens, etc.	1940–44	PA/NC/5/53
Detention orders re British Union of Fascist members	1940–43	PA/NC/5/58
Sunderland Borough Council war refugees	1940–42	T170/30

Warwickshire

County Record Office
Priory Park
Cape Road
Warwick CV34 4JS

Lists of Belgian refugees and wounded Belgian soldiers in Rugby Police Division	1914–15	CR2770
Details of aliens, Kingsbury Police beat	1940–53	CR2770
Details of aliens, Mappleborough Police beat	1935–54	CR2770
Details of aliens, Wolston Police beat	1931–55	CR2770
Details of aliens, Baginton Police beat	1935–54	CR2770

West Midlands

Birmingham Libraries
Central Library
Chamberlain Square
Birmingham B3 3HQ

Belgian refugee register	1915	ZZ34 302724
Registration forms completed by Belgian refugees on arrival at the receiving home in Islington Row, Birmingham	1916–18	MS 652/2

West Midlands Police Museum
Sparkhill Police Station
Stratford Road
Sparkhill
Birmingham B11 4EA

Aliens registration cards	1914–	37/100
Register of aliens	1914–	38/102
Aliens day book	1914–	38/103
Casual aliens register	1914–18	38/104

Worcestershire

Worcestershire Record Office
City Centre Branch
St Helen's Church
Fish Street
Worcester WR1 2HN

Register of Belgians and minute book of committee of refugees, Worcester City Archives	1913	shelf C2

West Mercia Constabulary
Police Heritage Centre
Hindlip Hall
Hindlip
PO Box 55
Worcester WR3 8SP

Index to register of Irishmen residing   1941–4   S Cdi
   in Oswestry Division

East Yorkshire

Archives and Records Service
County Hall
Beverley, East Riding of Yorkshire HU17 9BA

East Riding Constabulary: alien cards   1938–42, 1945   Acc. 2020A
East Riding Constabulary: index to   c. 1948   Acc. 1671
   registers of aliens

Hull City Archives
79 Lowgate
Hull, HU1 1HN

Aliens certificates   1793–1815   BRE/7
Material relating to the investigation   1865–88   BHH 1/48–59; TCM
   of sickness, death and other health   172–181; WHG 1/20–46
   issues on immigrant ships
Coroner's inquests into deaths on   1840–99   CQB
   immigrant ships
Papers relating to anti-German riots   1915   CW/2/12
Minutes and papers of the Greek   1886   TCM & TCGG
   Gypsies Committee

West Yorkshire

Bradford District Archives
15 Canal Road
Bradford BD1 4AT

Bradford Birkerend Immigrant Centre: 1965–75   18D80
   admission registers and attendance
   records

Kirklees District Archives
Central Library
Princess Alexandra Walk
Huddersfield HD1 2SU

Lists of aliens at Stonyhurst school   1803   DD/WBL/116/27
Belgian refugees committee,   1919   KC 65
   Netherton: correspondence
Huddersfield County Borough,   1937–53   KA 165
   Spanish Relief Fund and War
   Refugees Fund, accounts
Huddersfield and District Council of   1977–81   KC859/7
   Churches file concerning the
   resettlement of Vietnamese refugees

Alphabetical list of refugees from Guernsey in Huddersfield	1940	KC825/2/2

Leeds District Archives
Chapeltown Road
Sheepscar
Leeds LS7 3AP

Leeds Jewish Refugees Committee	1939–50	

West Yorkshire Police Archive Service
Newstead Road
Wakefield WF1 2DE

West Riding Constabulary: aliens – register of foreigners summoned	1948–53	A299/85
West Riding Constabulary: aliens – register of foreigners summoned	1953–65	A299/86
Halifax Borough Police: notebook recording illegal aliens	1958–64	A366/27
Halifax Borough Police: certificates of illegal aliens (2 items)	1955	A366/28
Halifax Borough Police: registration cards of illegal aliens (2 items)	1947 and 1956	A366/29

South Yorkshire

Doncaster Archives
King Edward Road
Doncaster DN4 0NA

Doncaster County Borough, Belgian refugee committee minutes, including the names of some of the refugees	1914–19	AB/2/2/10

Wales

Carmarthenshire

Carmarthenshire Archive Service
Parc Myrddin
Richmond Terrace
Carmarthen SA31 1DS

Letter book of the Distress Committee for aiding Belgian refugees	1914–15	CAC/RC
General history of the Belgian refugee movement in the Carmarthen Union	1915	CAS/Sc Bk XIII

Mayor of Carmarthen's War Relief Committee (Belgian Refugees Department)	1914–19	CAS/Sc Bk XII

Denbighshire

Denbighshire Record Office
46 Clwyd Street
Ruthin
Denbighshire LL15 1HP

Flintshire

County Record Office
The Old Rectory
Hawarden CH5 3NR

Register of aliens at Bryn Yorkin, Llanfynydd	1915	D/DM/294/22
Legal papers re anti-German riot at Rhyl in which immigrant's premises were damaged	1915–16	FC/C/4/2/29
Letter from Belgian refugees at Caerwys	1914	D/L/87
Account of Belgian refugees at Gredington, Hanmer	1914–15	NT/559
Notes on Belgian refugees sent to Holywell	1915	UD/C/1/76
Card of thanks from Belgian refugees at St Asaph	1915	PC/57/46

Glamorganshire

West Glamorgan Archive Service
County Hall
Oystermouth Road
Swansea SA1 3SN

Swansea Borough Police aliens registration cards	c. 1930–72	

Gwent

Gwent County Record Office
County Hall
Cwmbran
Gwent NP44 2XH

Report concerning Belgian refugees at Mathern Palace	1914	Misc. MSS 1487
Minute book, accounts and correspondence concerning the Belgian refugee relief in Machen	1914–17	D314.45–7

Gwent Constabulary
Croesyceiliog
Cwmbran
Gwent NP44 2XJ

Alien registration cards	1947–	

Pembrokeshire

Pembrokeshire Record Office
The Castle
Dew Street
Haverfordwest
Pembrokeshire SA61 1SU

War refugees (mainly Belgian) landing at Milford Haven	1940–46	PCC/SS/1/54

Appendix 3

Listing of certificates and declarations of naturalization and British nationality

Naturalization Act 1870: certificates of naturalization

Certificate A	Certificate (ordinary) to a person with five years' residence in the United Kingdom during the eight years immediately preceding application for naturalization
Certificate AA	Certificate to a person with five years' service under the Crown during the eight years immediately preceding application for naturalization
Certificate AAA	Certificate to a person in the Diplomatic or Consular Service with five years' service under the Crown during the eight years immediately preceding application for naturalization
Certificate B	Certificate to a person who has already been granted a certificate of naturalization under the act of 1844
Certificate C	Certificate to a person of 'doubtful nationality', with five years' residence in the United Kingdom, or five years' service under the Crown, during the eight years immediately preceding application for re-admission
Certificate D	Certificate of re-admission of person to British nationality with five years' residence in the United Kingdom, or five years' service under the Crown, during the last eight years immediately preceding application for re-admission
Certificate DA	Certificate granted by Governor of any British possession and registered in the the Home Office, or re-admission of person with five years' residence in that possession, or with five years' service under the Crown, during the eight years immediately preceding application for re-admission

Naturalization Act 1870: declarations of alienage

Declaration E	Declaration by a person, a subject of a foreign state subsequently naturalized as a British subject, renouncing British nationality
Declaration F	Declaration by a person, an alien by origin but born within HM dominions, renouncing British nationality
Declaration G	Declaration by a person, born out of HM dominions to a father being a British subject, renouncing British nationality

Naturalization Act 1870: declarations of British nationality

Declaration H	Declaration by a natural-born British subject, renouncing subsequent naturalization in a foreign state

British Nationality and Status of Aliens Act 1914: certificates of naturalization

Certificate A and AZ	Certificate (ordinary) granted under Section 2 of the act, where the names of children are not included
Certificate B and BZ	Similar to Certificate A, but including the names of children
Certificate C and CZ	Certificate granted under sub-section (2) of Section 5 of the act to a minor
Certificate D	Special certificate granted under Section 4 of the act to a person with respect to whose nationality a doubt exists, where the names of children are not included
Certificate DZ	Certificate of naturalization granted to a woman who was at birth a British subject and is married to a subject of a state at war with His Majesty
Certificate E	Similar to Certificate D, but including the names of children
Certificate EZ	Similar to Certificate DZ, but including the names of children
Certificate F	Certificate granted under Section 6 of the act to a person naturalized before the passing of the act, where the names of children are not included
Certificate G	Similar to Certificate F, but including the names of children
Certificate GZ	Similar to Certificate FZ, but including the names of children
Certificate M	Special Certificate granted under Section 4 of the act to a person with respect to whose nationality a doubt exists
Certificate O	Certificate granted under Section 8 of the act by the government of a British possession overseas

British Nationality Act 1948: certificates of British nationality

Certificate BNA	Application made by a subject of a foreign state resident in the UK
Certificate M	s7 & 18 1948 act: application for registration of a minor child
Certificate O	Application made by a subject of a foreign state resident overseas
Certificate R1	s6(1) 1948 act: application made by an adult British subject or citizen of the Republic of Ireland, or any of the Channel Islands, Isle of Man, a colony, a protectorate or a protected state to which s8(1) of the act applied, or a UK Trust Territory, or on the grounds of Crown Service under HM Government in the UK
Certificate R2	s6 (2) 1948 act: application made by a woman who has been married to a citizen of the UK and colonies
Certificate R3	s6 (2) 1948 act: application made by a woman who has been married to a citizen of the UK and colonies
Certificate R4	s12 (6) 1948 act: application made by a person who but for his citizenship or potential citizenship of one of the countries mentioned in s1 (3) of the act would have become a citizen of the UK and colonies under s12 (4) of the act
Certificate R5	s16 1948 act: application to resume British nationality by a person who has ceased to be a British subject on the loss of British nationality by his father or mother in accordance with s12 (1) of the 1914 act
Certificate R6	s19 1948 act: declaration of citizenship made by a citizen of the UK and colonies who is also a citizen of one of the countries mentioned in s13 of the act or of the Republic of Ireland or a national of a foreign country

Appendix 4

Useful addresses and websites

Anglo-German Family History Society, 14 River Reach, Teddington, Middlesex TW11 9QL. Web site: http://www.feefhs.org

The Bevis Marks Hall, 2 Heneage Lane, London EC3A 5DQ.

The Black Cultural Archives, 378 Coldharbour Lane, London SW9 8LF.

The Black Genealogical Society, 10 Hey Park, Liverpool, Merseyside L36 6HR.

Borthwick Institute, St Anthony's Hall, Peasholme Green, York YO1 7PW. Tel: 01904 642315.

British Library, 96 Euston Road, London NW1 2DB. Tel: 020 7412 7677.

The Chief Rabbi's Office, Adler House, 735 High Road, North Finchley, London N12 0US

French Protestant Church of London, Soho Square, London.

Hartley Library, Special Collections, University of Southampton, Highfield, Southampton SO17 1BJ. Tel: 023 80592721.

Home Office, Record Management Services, 50 Queen Anne's Gate, London SW1 9AH.

House of Lords Record Office, House of Lords, London SW1A 0PW. Tel: 020 7219 5316.

Huguenot Library, University College, Gower Street, London WC1E 6BT. Tel: 020 7380 7094.

Immigration and Nationality Department, Liverpool Nationality Office, B4 Division, India Buildings, Water Street, Liverpool L2 0QN.

Institute of Commonwealth Studies, 28 Russell Square, London WC1B 5DS. Tel: 020 7580 5876.

International Council of the Red Cross, Archives Division, 19 Ave de la Paix, CH-1202 Geneva, Switzerland.

Jewish Genealogical Society of Great Britain, PO Box 13288, London N3 3WB. Web site: http://www.jgsgb.ort.org

Jewish Refugees Committee, Drayton House, Gordon Street, London WC1H. Tel: 020 7387 4747.

Liverpool Nationality Office see Immigration and Nationality Department.

London Metropolitan Archives, 40 Northampton Road, London EC1R 0HB. Tel: 020 7332 3820.

Manchester Local Studies Unit, Central Library, St Peter's Square, Manchester M2 5PD. Tel: 0161 234 1959.

Manx Heritage Library, Kingswood Drive, Douglas, Isle of Man IM1 3LY. Tel: 01624 648000.

Oriental and India Office Collections, The British Library, 96 Euston Road, London NW1 2DB. Tel: 020 73237353

P & O Ferries Group, Information Department, Peninsular House, 79 Pall Mall, London SW1Y 5EJ. Tel: 020 7930 4343.

Polish Institute and Sikorski Museum, Archives Department, 20 Princes Gate, London SW7 1PT. Tel: 020 7589 9249.

The Polish Library, 238–246 King Street, London W6 0RF. Tel: 020 8741 0474.

Westminster Abbey Muniments Room and Library, London SW1P 3PA. Tel: 020 7222 5152.

For Caribbean ancestry: http://www.rootsweb.com/~caribgw

For Jewish ancestry: http://www.jewishgen.org

For the location of historical manuscripts and papers outside the Public Records: http://www.hmc.gov.uk

Bibliography

C. Andrew, *The Security Service 1908–1945* (PRO, London, 1999)

A. Bevan, *Tracing Your Ancestors in the Public Record Office* 5th edn (PRO, London, 1999)

J. L. Boulton (Ed) *The Alien Communities of London in the Fifteenth Century: The Subsidy Rolls of 1440 and 1483–4.* (Paul Watkins, Stamford, 1998)

W. Cunningham, *Alien Immigration to Britain* (London, 1897, reprint Allen and Unwin, 1969)

J. Gibson, *Quarter Sessions Records for Family Historians* (FFHS, Birmingham, 1995)

G. Grannum, *Tracing Your West Indian Ancestors* (PRO, London, 1995)

C. Holmes, *John Bull's Island: Immigration and British Society 1871–1971* (Macmillan, London, 1988).

C. Jones, *Immigration and Social Policy* (Tavistock, London, 1977)

Z. Layton-Henry, *The Politics of Immigration* (Oxford, Blackwell, 1992)

N. Merriman (Ed) *The Peopling of London: Fifteen Thousand Years of Settlement from Overseas* (Museum of London, 1993)

K. Smith, C. T. Watts and M. J. Watts, *Records of Merchant Shipping and Seamen* (PRO, London, 1998)

A. Thurston, *Sources for Colonial Studies in the Public Record Office* (HMSO, London, 1995)

J. Walvin, *The Black Presence: A Documentary History of the Negro in England, 1555–1860* (London, 1971)

J. Walvin, *Black and White: The Negro in English Society, 1555–1945* (London, 1973)

J. Walvin, *Passage to Britain* (Penguin, London, 1984)

Index